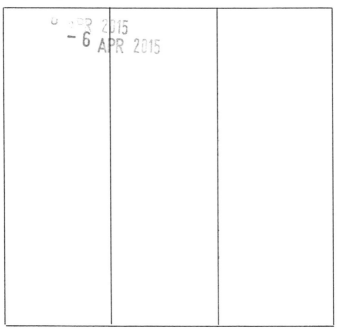

APOLLINAIRE
in the Great War
1914–1918

DAVID HUNTER

PETER OWEN
London and Chicago

PETER OWEN PUBLISHERS
81 Ridge Road, London N8 9NP

Peter Owen books are distributed in the USA and Canada
by Independent Publishers Group / Trafalgar Square
814 North Franklin Street, Chicago, IL 60610, USA

First published in English in Great Britain
by Peter Owen Publishers 2015

PAPERBACK ISBN 978-0-7206-1601-9
EPUB ISBN 978-0-7206-1644-6
MOBIPOCKET ISBN 978-0-7206-1646-0
PDF ISBN 978-0-7206-1647-7

A catalogue record for this book is available from the British Library

Printed and bound in the UK by
CPI Group (UK) Ltd, Croydon, CR0 4YY

In memory of Madina Niang
Vive et preste comme un oiseau

ACKNOWLEDGEMENTS

Many people have contributed to this publication. Jacqueline Peltier, ably seconded by her husband Max, has been a constant source of support and advice, drawing on her own research on Apollinaire's war years. I would particularly like to thank her for working with me on many of the translations in the book. Peter Read and Laurence Campa, as well as providing inspiring examples of Apollinaire scholarship, have been very generous in answering questions about the poet's life and writings. Indeed, I should pay homage to the many scholars and enthusiasts whose primary research has provided the basis for this book, especially the group that meets in Paris every November (along with Jacqueline Apollinaire's relatives) to commemorate the poet's death and which is presided over by the wonderfully knowledgeable Claude Debon. Among friends, I would especially like to thank Colin Bailey for his close reading of the text and Richard Mason for his suggestions about my poetry translations. At my publishers, Antonia Owen and her colleagues have been unfailingly responsive and helpful. Finally, I owe a great debt to my wife Oonagh Gay for her comments on my draft and to my daughters Catriona and Mairead for putting up with many years of chatter about Apollinaire. Catriona also employed her design skills to produce the map and a couple of the picture poems featured in the book.

I am particularly grateful to Beverley Bie Brahic and CB Editions for allowing me to use a range of her translations of Apollinaire's wartime poems from her collection *The Little Auto*. The individual poems are highlighted in my endnotes. I would also like to thank the University of California Press for their permission to reproduce Anne Hyde Greet's translations of 'On arrival from Dieuze', 'Cotton in Your Ears' and 'Aim'. Stephen Romer has also very kindly allowed me to print his translation 'My Lou Tonight I Shall Sleep in the Trenches'. All the other translations, both of poems and Apollinaire's prose correspondence, are mine in collaboration with Jacqueline Peltier. Any mistakes or omissions, of course, remain my responsibility.

CONTENTS

ILLUSTRATIONS
between pages 128 and 129

Apollinaire's mother Angelica in 1899
Apollinaire and the artist André Rouveyre in Paris on
    1 August 1914
Louise de Coligny-Châtillon (Lou) in 1914
Apollinaire with comrades at the Champagne front, 1915
Yves Blanc, Apollinaire's 'war godmother'
A sentry in a front-line trench in the Champagne region,
    1915–16
Map of the Champagne front April–December 1915
Map of the Champagne front January–March 1916
Apollinaire with Madeleine Pagès in Algeria, January 1916
Apollinaire drawn by Picasso, 1916
Apollinaire at the Conservatoire Renée Maubel before the
    première of *Les Mamelles de Tirésias* in Paris, June 1917
Apollinaire with his wife Jacqueline at the 'pigeon loft',
    202, boulevard Saint-Germain, in 1917 or 1918

PRELUDE:
PARIS
1914

By mid-1914 Paris could legitimately claim to be the artistic centre of Europe, if not the world. Innovations in harmony, rhythm and form introduced by Fauré, Debussy and Ravel had placed French composers at the forefront of modern music, while the unique sound-realm created by Satie was inspiring his younger contemporaries. The Paris seasons of Diaghilev's Ballets Russes brought together choreographers, musicians, designers and dancers in groundbreaking artistic collaborations such as *The Rite of Spring*, unveiled at a stormy première in the previous year. In 1913, too, Proust had published the first volume of *À la recherche du temps perdu*. And France remained home to most of the leading visual artists of the time, not least Pablo Picasso.

At the heart of this creative ferment – indeed of a network of contacts that by 1914 stretched across Europe and beyond – was the author, poet and critic Wilhelm de Kostrowitzky, better known by his pen name of Guillaume Apollinaire. Born in Rome in 1880 of an unknown father and a domineering mother of Polish origins, Angelica, Apollinaire had led a rootless early life during which periods of stability that enabled him to gain some education and make lifelong friends – at school in Monaco between 1888 and 1895, for instance – had been punctuated by others when the young man and his younger brother Albert had been dragged in Angelica's wake around different towns and cities of Europe, while she made a shadowy living, often as a casino hostess.

By the early 1900s, however, Apollinaire had settled perma-
nently in Paris and, while working in various banks, had begun to
take his first steps towards making his name as a journalist with an
interest in a wide variety of contemporary topics but particularly
in avant-garde painting. Friendship with the young Pablo Picasso,
whom he first met in 1905 and about whose work he published an
article in that same year, as well as his extensive contacts with many
other leading avant-garde artists, would eventually put Apollinaire
in the forefront of the debates and controversies around cubism –
debates that were still vigorous in 1913 when he published his
Méditations esthétiques: Les Peintres cubistes (*Aesthetic Meditations:
The Cubist Painters*). He and Picasso remained close for the rest of
Apollinaire's life, acting as witnesses at each other's marriages in
1918.

But art criticism was not his only interest. The young man had
also nurtured serious literary ambitions since his teenage years. He
published his first poems in literary reviews during 1901 and his
first short stories in 1902 before starting up his own short-lived
magazine, *Le Festin d'Ésope*, in 1903. His first book, *L'Enchanteur
pourrissant* (*The Rotting Magician*), appeared in 1909, a strange
conversation between the dead Merlin and a range of mythological
and biblical figures, illustrated by André Derain.[1] A collection of
short stories, *L'Hérésiarque et Cie.* (*The Heresiarch and Co.*),
followed in 1910 and was nominated for the prestigious Goncourt
literary prize. A year later Apollinaire completed *Le Bestiaire ou
Cortège d'Orphée* (*The Bestiary or Orpheus's Procession*), brief poems
meditating on the symbolic and personal significance of different
animals, interspersed with verses on Orpheus, this time with illustrations by Raoul Dufy.

However, it was Apollinaire's final publication before the war,
a major volume of poetry entitled *Alcools* that appeared in 1913,
which established him as a radically new voice in French verse.

Many of the poems sang of lost love and, in particular, of Apollinaire's doomed affairs with Annie Playden – a young English-woman he had met in 1901 when he was engaged as tutor and she as governess for the daughter of the German-born vicomtesse de Milhau – and with the French painter Marie Laurencin, who had been his companion between 1907 and 1912. But, while the overall tone of the volume was lyrical, the poet daringly suppressed all punctuation and combined everyday life, myth and religion (Apollinaire had been very devout as a boy), invective and elegy, traditional French metres and free verse in poems of striking modernity, such as 'Zone'. By 1914, then, Apollinaire was clearly a coming man in literary circles and was full of plans for the future.

The Great War shattered this world and plunged Apollinaire and many of his colleagues in the artistic avant-garde into a conflict that was unprecedented in its scope, violence and horror. It was also the first major war on European soil in which a high proportion of the soldiers involved in the fighting were literate. Post was free for men serving in the French Army, and the conscripts took full advantage of this opportunity. Apollinaire himself sent and received an extraordinary volume of letters during the war, primarily to two young women, Louise de Coligny and Madeleine Pagès. These letters describe at length his experiences as a soldier, both in training and on the front line, woo and cajole his wartime lovers, comment on artistic trends – including his own poetic practice – and contain a wide range of poems written at the front. Often including small drawings in the margin, the letters in many ways represent creative acts in their own right.

While some aspects of this correspondence will come as little surprise to readers familiar with English-language accounts of the war – trench warfare was equally murderous for all the belligerents – the letters point up significant and, at times, unexpected differences in the French experience, a consequence of France's distinct military traditions, the political and social context of the war for the country (after all, large swathes of its land area and a significant percentage of its population were under German occupation between 1914 and 1918) and even the geology of the areas of the front line contested by French troops.

Meanwhile, throughout the war Apollinaire continued to produce poetry, prose and plays that were profoundly marked by his involvement in the conflict. But, unlike many of the British poets who came to maturity during the war, Apollinaire was a fully fledged artist aged thirty-four by the time he enlisted; an artist, moreover, who differed from his English-speaking counterparts both in the literary tradition he would call upon – he was steeped in the French classics but had also been a great reader of chivalric romances in his youth and later edited works by de Sade and other authors of erotica – and in his ability to deploy, as a result of his previous work, the full panoply of modernist literary approaches and techniques in order to capture the experience of modern war.

In drawing so extensively on Apollinaire's correspondence and his works in prose and poetry, therefore, this book seeks not only to tell one man's fascinating and ultimately heart-rending story but to present a different, perhaps at times shocking, perspective for English-language readers who have grown up with a particular set of assumptions about the Great War and the literature it produced. At a time when historians seem to agree on the global nature of the conflict – and many countries are commemorating its centenary at the time of writing – but when popular and political debates around the causes, meaning and consequences of the war often remain narrowly focused along national lines, exploring such alternative views is surely as important as ever.

POSTLUDE:
PARIS
NOVEMBER 1918

'Si je mourais là-bas sur le front de l'armée'
– Guillaume Apollinaire, Nîmes, 30 January 1915

In the end he didn't die out there, at the front, despite having served on one of the most murderous theatres of the war.

November promised to be a busy month. His latest play, *Couleur du temps* (*Colour of Time*), had been cleared by the censors and was now in rehearsal, its première scheduled for the 24th. Luckily he had managed to persuade his friend, the artist Vlaminck, to paint the sets, replacing the original designer, whose translating duties with the US forces in France had become overwhelming. As always there was a profusion of other literary projects to complete – novels, poems, articles, film scripts, even a comic opera – while his military duties at the Ministry for the Colonies and his work for various journals continued to take up more time than he would have wished.

On 3 November he met his fellow poet Blaise Cendrars, who took him off to lunch and gave him a tube of Haarlem Oil, a sulphurous concoction dating from the Middle Ages and reputed to have powerful medicinal properties.[1] The fever began soon afterwards, and in the days that followed the influenza engulfed him. Friends came and went and came back again, Picasso and Max Jacob included, their mood ever darker. Dr Capmas, Cocteau's physician, was called but could do nothing. In many ways the poet had been lucky, missing the deadly early months of the war and the charnel-house of Verdun. He had survived a shrapnel wound to the head, trepanning and several bouts of hospitalization to clear his gas-torn lungs of congestion. But this time he would not escape death. No one knew the exact origins of the virus – some thought it had been brought back from Asia by Spanish sailors or blamed the recent influx of US troops into Europe, while others suspected the Germans of waging bacteriological warfare – but its effects were devastating. Around a quarter of a million are thought to have succumbed in France alone, some twenty million worldwide; he was one of many.[2]

He died at five o'clock in the evening on Saturday 9 November in his tiny rooftop flat – the 'pigeon loft' – at 202, boulevard Saint-Germain. It was 1918, just two days before the armistice that would end the Great War in which he had fought bravely and to which he had borne witness extensively, if often obliquely, in his poetry and prose. Picasso was too grief-stricken to act, leaving Cocteau to notify friends and to arrange notices in the newspapers. Louise Faure-Favier dressed the dead poet in his military uniform, placed a crucifix between his hands and his kepi by his side.[3]

In the days that followed flowers and mourners arrived in profusion at the flat, including the poet's mother and her long-term companion, Jules Weil, both incongruously dressed for a wedding they had been on their way to attend. The formidable Angelica, according to one account, berated the deceased's wife Jacqueline for not letting her know earlier about her son's illness, as if by sheer force of will she could have prevented his death.[4] Outside, if other reports are to be believed, the revellers celebrating victory in the streets chanted '*À bas Guillaume*' ('Down with William'). The William in question was Kaiser Wilhelm II, but the anecdote resonated for a poet who had styled himself *le mal-aimé* (the ill-loved one).

Four days later, on the 13th, the poet's body was carried via the church of St Thomas d'Aquin, where he had married Jacqueline only six months before, to Père-Lachaise Cemetery in eastern Paris. The cortège following the coffin through the still crowded streets included many of the city's leading artistic and literary figures – Picasso, Max Jacob, André Salmon, Cocteau, Paul Fort, Léger and other friends. A section of the 237th Territorial Regiment ensured that the poet was accorded full military honours, as befitted an officer who, despite his wounds, was still part of France's military establishment, had been awarded a *Croix de Guerre* and would be given a retrospective promotion to first lieutenant a few days after his death.[5] He entered the army records as '*Mort pour la France*'.

And so was buried Guglielmo Alberto Wladimiro Alessandro Apollinare de Kostrowitzky (the name registered shortly after his birth), Wilhelm to his mother and brother, Kostro or Guillaume to his friends, Cointreau-Whisky to the more linguistically inventive of his comrades at the front, Gui to his wartime lovers and Apollinaire to the world of poetry. He was by no means the only writer to die during the war – some five hundred have their names inscribed on the wall of the Panthéon in Paris – but he was certainly one of the most significant.[6]

In a poem written in late January 1915, shortly before he transferred to the front, 'Si je mourais là-bas' ('If I Were to Die Out There'), Apollinaire captured a mood common among French soldiers at the time: their premonitions of death and fear of being forgotten; the heightened eroticism engendered by wartime conditions; the hope that their sacrifice would create a better world.

> If I were to die out there at the front
> You'd cry for a while o Lou my beloved
> And then my memory would fade just as a shell
> Exploding dies out there at the front
> A lovely shell like mimosa in flower
>
> And then this memory shattered in the ether
> Would cover the whole world with my blood

Seas mountains valleys and the passing star
Wonderful suns ripening in the ether
Just like the golden fruits around Baratier

A forgotten memory living in all things
I would redden the tips of your pretty pink breasts
I would redden your mouth and your blood-red hair
You would not grow old all these beautiful things
Would grow younger again for their amorous ends

The deadly spurting of my blood on the world
Would give to the sun a much brighter sheen
More colour to the flowers more speed to the wave
An incredible love would descend on the world
The lover would be stronger in your spread-eagled body

Lou if I die out there a memory that's forgotten
– Remember from time to time in your moments of madness
Of youth and of love and of burning passion –
My blood is the burning fountain of bliss
And be the happiest of women since you're the prettiest

O my one true love and my great folly

Night descends
One can foresee
A long and bloody destiny[7]

The poet becomes, by his art, both ubiquitous and immortal, themes that run throughout Apollinaire's work and will reoccur in much his war poetry.

And the years since his death can be said to have proved him right. Apollinaire's influence is well attested: as an author inspiring succeeding generations of poets both in France and elsewhere; as a journalist and art critic championing cubism and inventing the term surrealism; as a collaborator and friend who remained a constant presence for Picasso and other major twentieth-century figures.[8] Indeed, perhaps the one area of his life that has only recently come to be fully explored and re-evaluated is his war service and writings.[9]

This is the story of Apollinaire during the years 1914 to 1918. It is a chronicle of military training and frontline soldiering, of two highly charged love affairs – one intensely physical, the other almost exclusively epistolary – and of a modernist poet and writer struggling courageously to create an individual and unique body of work from the collective experience of a machine-dominated and cataclysmic war. It is the one man's tale, but at the same time it offers us a French perspective on the Great War that in many ways contrasts with British views and representations of the conflict.[10]

Even in death Apollinaire challenges us.

1
DEAUVILLE, PARIS, NICE
AUGUST–DECEMBER 1914

The final days of peace found Apollinaire not in Paris but at the fashionable seaside resort of Deauville. He and a colleague, the graphic artist André Rouveyre, had arrived at the Hôtel de l'Europe in the early evening of 26 July 1914 with a commission to cover the summer season on behalf of the journal *Comœdia*. Apollinaire was to provide the anecdotes and Rouveyre to illustrate them.

Apollinaire chronicled the short period that he and Rouveyre spent in Deauville and their ensuing journey back to Paris in both prose and poetry, an indication of how significant he felt these few hours had been in his life. An initial article, handed in to *Comœdia* on 1 August (but not published in the journal until 1920), was later extended to form part of a longer novel, *La Femme blanche des Hohenzollern* (*The White Woman of the Hohenzollerns*), which remained unfinished at the poet's death.[1]

The first chapter of this manuscript, which draws heavily on Apollinaire's journal article and is entitled 'La Fête manquée ou le Miracle de la mobilisation' ('The Missed Party or the Miracle of the Mobilization'), imaginatively recreates the final days of peace and the first days of war. Initially there is little concern in Deauville's hotels and casino about the political tensions of late July 1914: 'No one believed the situation would become serious.' But as the poet and the illustrator mingle with the artistic, literary and society figures gathered at the resort (the poet makes sure to list the names and salient features of the guests, as the readers of *Comœdia* would no doubt have expected) they become aware of a growing disquiet.[2]

And there are strange goings-on, presaging the coming cataclysm. A black man in a brightly coloured costume cycles down to the sea and seems to sink into it, his sea-green turban mingling with waves. A large German woman, apparently without her official documents, becomes hysterical at the prospect of imprisonment or death at the hands of the French, until shuffled off-stage by a beautiful and mysterious acquaintance who hints at the existence of extensive Teutonic spy networks. Apollinaire and Rouveyre take the precaution of filling up their car with petrol.

Late in the evening of 31 July, the day before the official opening of the season, having received news that mobilization is imminent, the pair set off on the road back to Paris. Rouveyre's driver, Nolent, is at the wheel. There is a puncture at Lisieux, and when they pull up under a streetlamp the light promptly goes out – another omen of war for Rouveyre. Another puncture and another stop, at which point they see a 'marvellous and unforgettable' sunrise over the Seine, which Apollinaire describes in a very lyrical passage: 'Black bars swim in opaline, purifying white, then a thousand dark celestial animals take on a purple hue, the stars grow pale, a deep, clear fire gilds the horizon.'

The day heats up rapidly 'as if Cupid himself were the fire-raiser', and the poet feels 'the infinite emptiness of my heart'. More prosaically, the brutal sunshine sends the travellers to sleep, and the car almost ends up in a ditch. Signs of the coming conflict abound. All the farriers have been woken up and marched off during the night; Versailles is full of troops in field dress; the socialist leader, Jean Jaurès, has been assassinated by a French nationalist. After a detour to Rouveyre's house at Fontainebleau they reach Paris. The evening papers are announcing the mobilization, and the first official posters are already appearing.[3]

The poet spends the night with friends, all of whom except him are being called up.[4] After his second sleepless night he tumbles out on to the streets accompanied by a small group of women who gradually disperse. He meets another friend who will later die a 'hero' on the Champagne front. Despite the widespread belief that the war will be short, he foresees a long struggle, an opinion underlined by a memoir from the Revolutionary and Napoleonic periods that he picks up by chance in a bookseller's and which talks of twenty-five years of war. The poet has in any case decided to join up and realizes he will have plenty of time to participate in 'the long and heroic party that would replace the party we missed at Deauville'.

The manuscript of *La Femme blanche* provides a good introduction to Apollinaire's literary strategies during the war. Auto-biographical fact and fantasy are artfully combined in ways that ground the poet's writing in lived experience yet allow plenty of scope for a poetic reimagination of his raw material. Even the facts are carefully chosen. The manuscript makes no mention, for instance, of the visit that Apollinaire and Rouveyre made to a photographic studio on the afternoon of 1 August which resulted in a remarkable sequence of animated photographs that can be viewed on the internet: Apollinaire tired but jovial and visibly enjoying himself; Rouveyre equally jovial but more self-conscious and clearly the junior partner.[5]

The transformation of experience is even more apparent in the free-verse poem 'La Petite auto' ('The Little Auto'), which takes as its core the journey back from Deauville to Paris and which was published in the collection *Calligrammes* in April 1918. Once again there is a thread of autobiographical detail: the evening departure from Deauville; the journey through Lisieux and Versailles; the punctures; the arrival in Paris as the mobilization is announced. It has even been suggested that the visual image in the shape of a car that sits at the centre of the poem is deliberately less complicated than similar images in other poems in order to mirror Rouveyre's 'little auto'. Also integrated into the text are allusions to specific areas of the Belgian Ardennes, where Apollinaire spent part of his youth, and to the progress of the war, from the German invasion to the beginnings of aerial combat.[6]

On the 31st of the month of August 1914
I left Deauville not long before midnight
In Rouveyre's little auto

Counting his chauffeur there were three of us

We bid farewell to a whole era
Furious giants were rising up over Europe
Eagles were leaving their aeries waiting for the sun
Voracious fish were swimming up from the abysses
Peoples came running to get to know one another better
The dead were shaking with fear in their dark dwellings

Dogs were barking over where the borders were
I left carrying with me inside me all those armies that were fighting
I could feel them rising inside me and rolling out the lands their
    columns were snaking through
With the forests the happy villages of Belgium
Francorchamps with Eau Rouge the Red River and the pouhons springs
The region the invasions have always passed through
Railroad arteries where those who were marching off to die
Saluted life's colours one last time
Deep oceans where monsters were shuddering
Among the ancient shipwreck carcasses
Unimaginable heights where man fights

Higher than the eagle can soar

Man fights man up there

And falls without warning like a shooting star

Inside me I could feel some dexterous new beings

Building and also furnishing a new universe

A merchant of unbelievable opulence and prodigious size

Was setting out his fabulous wares

And gigantic shepherds were leading

Huge dumb flocks that were grazing on the speeches

And along the road all the dogs were barking at them

I shall never forget this journey by night during which none of us said a word

O		
so	O	
mbre	tender	O
departure	night	vil
when our 3	of before	lages
headlights died	the war	towards

which hurried

BLACKSMITHS RECALLED

BETWEEN MIDNIGHT AND ONE IN THE MORNING

n		v
ear	or maybe	ers
LISIEUX		ailles the
the very		gold
blue		en

and 3 times we stopped to change a popped tyre

And when after having passed that afternoon

Through Fontainebleau

We arrived in Paris

Just as they were posting the mobilization orders

We understood my comrade and I

That the little auto had driven us into a New Era

And although we were both already grown men

We had just been born

However, the poet reshapes these elements in very significant ways. Distance from the events of late July and early August 1914 – the first draft of the poem is believed to have been written several months afterwards and the central section later still – allows Apollinaire to develop an apocalyptic vision of the war in which creatures from the depths of the oceans to the heights of the heavens are stirred and even the dead in their graves are afraid. The poet becomes a seer, able to span both time and space, foreseeing and nurturing within himself the new world that the war will create.[7] The very first line of the poem changes the timing of the adventure with Rouveyre from 31 July to 31 August, creating links to popular songs of the period but also aligning the journey to the date in 1880 on which the Apollinaire's birth was first declared to the authorities in Rome – a way of emphasizing the rebirth occasioned by the conflict.[8]

In order to participate fully in this brave new world, however, the poet would have to join up. This was to prove more difficult than he could have imagined.

Despite his importance as a writer and critic in the Parisian avant-garde, in August 1914 Apollinaire remained officially a foreigner, born in Rome of an unknown father and a mother of Polish origins and Russian by nationality. Within days of Germany's formal declaration of war on France on 3 August, friends such as the Italian Ricciotto Canudo and the Swiss Blaise Cendrars had begun joining units of the French Foreign Legion and were actively encouraging other foreign nationals to do likewise, but Apollinaire could have attempted to concentrate on his art (as Picasso chose to do) or to sit out the war in a neutral country.[9]

Instead, on 5 August, he presented himself at an auxiliary recruitment office for the literary community, opened in rue de

Vaugirard by the journal *Les Marches de l'Est* and conveniently close to the poet's flat. There he completed an enlistment form and submitted a request for naturalization as a French citizen.[10] However, these recruitment offices had no official status and any application to join up required ratification by the military authorities, whose official enlistment campaign was not due to start until the 21st of the month. The military authorities were, in any case, overwhelmed with the task of mobilization (as well as increasingly concerned about espionage) and were giving priority among volunteers wishing to join regular-army units to those with flying or mechanical experience. On 24 August Apollinaire learned that his application to enlist had been deferred. An appeal directly to the Ministry of Justice two days later had no effect.[11]

The poet was now in a difficult position. Most of his fellow artists and friends had been taken into the army or were scattered in other parts of France (Picasso, for instance, was in Avignon). Moreover, much of Paris was closed, including many of the journals and literary magazines upon which Apollinaire depended for his livelihood. Those publications that continued to appear were understandably devoting a great deal of their coverage to the war and little to the arts, particularly as, by late August, the German advance through Belgium and northern France was bringing the capital under direct threat. So when a friend, the lawyer and part-time man of letters Henry Siegler-Pascal, whose own mobilization as a territorial had been postponed, decided to join his brother in Nice and suggested that Apollinaire accompany him, the poet readily accepted. It would be a return to a region where he had spent a large part of his childhood and to a city whose *lycée* he had attended in the late 1890s.

Apollinaire left Paris on 3 September in the most difficult of circumstances and only after the director of the prestigious literary magazine *Mercure de France* had intervened with the authorities to secure official permission for the poet's journey. German cavalry was less than sixteen kilometres from Paris, and the French government had transferred to Bordeaux the previous day.[12] Some half a million people had already fled the capital, which was in a state of siege, and refugees continued to stream south from the northern war zones. Much of the railway network had been requisitioned for transporting troops, so, not surprisingly, the passage to Nice took several days – presaging other future long and difficult wartime train journeys for the poet – and it was not until 6 September that Apollinaire finally arrived at his destination.

It could be argued that Apollinaire's attempt to join up was prompted more by practical necessity than by any great commitment to the French cause. Certainly, the onset of war was devastating for the poet's finances, which were always precarious. In *Souvenirs de la Grande Guerre* (*Memories of the Great War*), a memoir that he began to prepare in late 1914 but which was never completed, the poet claimed that by the summer of that year his savings were almost exhausted, referring to 'my account at *Crédit Lyonnais* where I've only 180 francs left – that's my whole fortune'.[13] The projections for the period November 1914 to November 1915 looked much rosier, with more than ten thousand francs and 'a quiet year' in prospect, but the war put paid to all that. As Pierre Caizergues notes in his introduction to *Souvenirs*, financial security had hardly been glimpsed before it disappeared.[14] The very fact that Apollinaire lists this vanished income in such detail in the memoir underlines the extent to which its loss still rankled. Military service at least offered some form of security.

The position of foreign nationals living in Paris in the early days of the war was also far from comfortable. Under strict surveillance and unable to leave the city without a formal *laissez-passer*, their lives were increasingly regulated. As the Germans advanced there were attacks on foreign businesses and even a few lynchings of suspected spies in some parts of France. On 4 August Apollinaire had been successful in his application to the authorities in his local *arrondissement* for a residence permit, but he could expect his professional and personal activities to be severely restricted, and the threat of expulsion or internment would never be far away.

Finally, the war came at a crucial time emotionally for the poet. He was still recovering from the break-up of his intense five-year relationship with the painter Marie Laurencin, a love affair that had prompted some of the greatest and most melancholy poetry in his 1913 collection *Alcools*, including the future anthology piece 'Le Pont Mirabeau' ('Mirabeau Bridge'). Marie was now taking refuge in neutral Spain, having married the German baron and painter Otto von Wätjen in June 1914, which only made things worse.[15] The army might offer Apollinaire a welcome refuge from his emotional turmoil.

Apollinaire's practical reasons for trying to enlist are only part of the story, however. The poet's sense of honour and of his aristocratic and military lineage also came into play. The Kostrowicki family was, after all, minor nobility in Poland. Apollinaire's maternal grandfather, Apollinaris, was an artillery officer in the Russian Army and had been wounded in the head at the siege of Sebastopol in 1855. The poet's father, although unknown, was long rumoured to be an Italian army officer. André Rouveyre describes Apollinaire in his memoir of the poet as a *'pur chevalier'* ('a pure knight').[16]

And there were personal motivations for affirming his loyalty to France. In 1911 the poet had been caught up, with Picasso, in the bizarre episode of the theft of the *Mona Lisa*. Six years earlier Apollinaire had met a Belgian conman, Géry Pieret, with whom he had kept in touch and who occasionally lodged with the poet. In 1907 Pieret had managed to secrete two Iberian stone heads out of the Louvre and had sold them to Picasso. In May 1911 he stole another head, which he deposited at Apollinaire's flat for a while.

When the *Mona Lisa* disappeared at the end of August 1911 Pieret
– and, by implication, Apollinaire – came under suspicion. On 7
September the poet was incarcerated in La Santé prison as an
accomplice to the theft. If the poem he wrote there, 'À la Santé' ('In
La Santé'), is an accurate depiction of his mental state during his
five days of incarceration, Apollinaire came close to despair and
even to a breakdown:

> Take pity on my feeble reason
> And this despair that overwhelms it[17]

Certainly his whole future in Paris must have seemed under
threat, as the reactionary press subjected him to vicious attacks as a
foreigner. Although he was released on 12 September, having no case
to answer (not, however, before appearing handcuffed in front of a
judge), the experience clearly marked him and made him reflect on
his status as an outsider.[18] Letters in the following years suggest he was
considering seeking naturalization as a French citizen. What better
way to prove his commitment to the country that had welcomed
him and to fix a French identity than by seeking glory in its army?

There is one final consideration. Apollinaire and many of his
fellow artists in Paris did not see Germany as just an economic and
military power. Rather, it represented for them a particular sort of
culture – joyless, sentimental, materialistic, Protestant – which
seemed antithetical to all they admired.[19] These feelings are evident
in the poem 'À l'Italie' ('To Italy') which Apollinaire wrote in the
late summer of 1915 as an attempt to encourage Italy to declare
war on Germany and from which the following extract is taken:

Italy
You our mother and daughter almost a sister
Like you I have the quarter litre of plonk

To cheer me up

Which puts such a distance between us and the Hun

Like you I too have the flight of the partridge flocks of 75s

Like you I don't have that joyless Hun pride and I know how to laugh

I'm not overly sentimental like those people who go to extremes in their
actions not knowing how to amuse themselves

Our civilization has more finesse than the things they use

It goes beyond a comfortable life

And what's external in art and industry

Flowers are our children and not theirs

Even the fleur de lys that dies in the Vatican[20]

The conflict that began in 1914 was therefore perceived as a war
of civilizations in which Apollinaire and his comrades would be
fighting to preserve the intellectual and moral superiority of
France.[21] Many historians now argue that the outbreak of war was
met more with stoical resignation than wild enthusiasm in the
belligerent countries. Literary and artistic circles were, however,
among the keenest proponents of the conflict in its early days, seeing
the war as a chance to renew France's national spirit and reassert its
universal cultural mission.[22]

Thus it was hardly surprising that Apollinaire should try to
join up in early August, nor that he should renew his attempts later,
eventually, as we shall see, succeeding in entering the artillery in
December 1914. By then, however, Apollinaire's life had changed
dramatically. He had met Lou.

La comtesse Geneviève Marguerite Marie-Louise de Pillot de
Coligny-Châtillon (1881–1963) – called Loulou by her friends but
Lou by Apollinaire – held many attractions for the poet. For a start,
she came from an illustrious family and was a direct descendant of

Gaspard II de Coligny. Gaspard, whose statue adorned the Louvre, was Admiral of France in the sixteenth century and had featured in Dumas's novel *La Reine Margot* (*Queen Margot*). As Apollinaire wrote to a later correspondent, Lou was someone 'in whose veins runs the blood of Saint Louis'.[23] Yet she was also a thoroughly modern woman, a keen walker who had abandoned her corset and was one of the earliest women aviators.[24] Married to a baron at twenty-three after a strict upbringing, she had divorced eight years later in 1912 and had since led an independent life of high-society frivolity, casual drug-taking and short-lived affairs (although she was to remain attached to a faithful boyfriend, Gustave Louis Toutaint – 'Toutou' – during the time she knew Apollinaire).[25]

Above all, she had such *poetic* possibilities. In *The Great War and Modern Memory* Paul Fussell has explored the pastoral models that many British authors used in their writing about the conflict. Apollinaire, in contrast, was steeped in the tradition of chivalric romances, which had been an important part of his extraordinarily wide-ranging reading as a young man. Here, then, was a woman whose troubadour the poet could be and for whose favours he could go into battle as a medieval knight would enter the field. As he wrote in the first letter he ever sent to her, 'I hope for nothing more than that you should permit a poet who loves you more than life itself to choose you as his damsel and to call himself . . . your passionate servant.'[26]

They first met in late September 1914. On his arrival in Nice Apollinaire had moved into a small flat that Siegler-Pascal had found for him at 26, rue Cotta, quickly making contacts among the city's literary and artistic community. On Sunday 27 September the poet was lunching with the lawyer and a group of friends at one of Nice's finest inns, Bouttau, when they were joined by a vivacious and talkative young woman. Apollinaire was immediately entranced.

That evening he sat beside her at an opium-smoking party at the residence of Borie de la Merline, who held the official positions of Commissaire à l'inscription maritime et Commandant du front de mer (Commissar for Maritime Registration and Shore Commander) as well as being a sometime author.[27] Lou was thirty-three years old, living with Mémée (Edmée Dedons de Pierrefeu), a cousin of her ex-husband, at the sumptuous Villa Baratier in nearby Saint-Jean-Cap-Ferrat, acting as a volunteer nurse at the military hospital in the Hotel Ruhl in Nice, virtually penniless, sensual and capricious.[28] The very next day Apollinaire wrote declaring his love. It was the start of a correspondence that would last until January 1916 and would prompt the poet to send her over two hundred letters as well as numerous poems.

There are relatively few letters from the autumn of 1914, as the poet and his newly-found muse were living close to one another and taking trips out to local towns such as Grasse, Menton and Vence. But those that exist are fascinating in a number of respects. They offer, first of all, a glimpse of the protagonists' man-oeuvrings as they tried to negotiate the terms of their relationship. Apollinaire's first passionate declaration – 'Already love is in turn bringing me so low and raising me so high that I wonder if I have ever truly been in love until now' – was followed on 3 October by an equally extravagant statement of his newly awakened feelings: 'Until now, even when I thought I was in love I kept much of myself back and even when I thought I was suffering I wished above all for a quick end to my distress, whereas now I want it to continue for as long as life itself.' It appears that Lou has given him grounds for hope: 'You've told me that you would be susceptible to love.' But the poet has seen her only three times and, he hints, never alone.

By 14 October he was already becoming disconcerted by her flirting and did not want to be involved in her games. 'I would not like, if there are only three of us this evening, to act as an amorous barrier, a fortification.' She had kept him waiting on the previous day and had clearly proposed that they remain just friends. This sense of Lou keeping her distance is reinforced by Apollinaire's next letter, of 20 October, in which he chided her for using just her surname in a letter she had sent him: 'If you are frightened of compromising yourself by writing to me, don't sign the letters.'

An undated letter from the end of October or early November shows the poet trying to keep calm. He was aiming to be a dear friend, and Lou should not be surprised if he did not appear jealous. Underneath it all, however, he admitted to being 'more and more agitated'. During November there is evidence of Lou's own ups-and-downs. 'I've thought all day', Apollinaire wrote, 'about your charming gaiety and those sudden bouts of melancholy.' There are also references to the high jinks of her set – a scurrilous story about Mémée's behaviour was circulating in Niçois society.

On 29 November the poet offered a further and very tender declaration of his passion for Lou. 'Your image never leaves me, nor the sound of your voice, nor your lovely simple stories whose echo still resonates in me, awakening a thousand tender thoughts that were sleeping but now hold out their arms to you.' However, the letter made it clear that Apollinaire was contemplating a major change in his situation. In fact, he had asked Borie de la Merline to intercede on his behalf and to support a renewed application to join the army.

Two days later Apollinaire had reached rock bottom. 'I feel so unhappy that I wish Borie's attempts would come to fruition as soon as possible and I could leave.' He had no intention, he said, of taking advantage of the permission Lou had now given him to see other women. Finally, on Saturday 5 December, he informed her that he had finally managed to enlist and would leave the following day to join an artillery regiment in Nîmes.[29] But he was having second thoughts and was, if anything, in lower spirits than before. 'It's why I've been so sad today, deathly sad.'

The letters are, then, intensely moving and personal; at the same time, they contain many elements of literary performance. Lou becomes Apollinaire's creation – a being formed of words and poetry – and the letters are the means by which this creation is realized.[30]

From the beginning the poet adopted the pose of the *mal-aimé* that had characterized much of his previous poetry. 'As you can see, without wanting to I've taken the precautions of a desperate man, because after a giddy moment of hope I now hope for nothing.' The letters are peppered with classical and literary allusions: Lou's breasts are 'more worthy of being conquered by a hero than the golden apples guarded by the Hesperides';[31] she has cast a spell over him like 'another Mélusine', a water-spirit from European folklore. By his second letter he was offering her copies of his books as tokens of love and was already contemplating writing one specifically for her, a book which he imagined in the most extravagant terms: 'And no doubt inspired by such a violent passion, and since you are involved, just as delicate a spirit, I will write the book that of all my books is most full of that humanity which in my view is the only thing worthy of moving men and of being sought by a writer.' On 14 October he suggested they spend a literary evening together during which he would read her new things, tell her about a play he was writing, make up stories for her and ask her advice. All for a woman whose taste in poetry was highly conventional and who later acknowledged that she really had not really understood her suitor.

The 'literariness' of their relationship is underlined by the short poems that Apollinaire began to offer Lou during this period. These were no ordinary verses but, rather, what the poet called '*petit(s) poème(s) idéogrammatique(s)*' in one of his letters. Apollinaire had published his first example of a 'picture poem' – 'Lettre-Océan' ('Ocean-Letter') – in the June 1914 edition of his magazine *Les Soirées de Paris*.[32] Others followed in July. Now, on 8 October, he sent Lou short texts in the form of a fig, a carnation and an opium pipe. He later inscribed presentation copies of his books *L'Hérésiarque et Cie.* and *Alcools* with poems in the shape of a palm tree, a flask and a cross.[33]

The content of these poems is largely uncontroversial – images describing the beloved, declarations of the poet's infatuation, references to aspects of their life in Nice and discreet erotic symbols such as the fig. However, the graphic qualities of the texts, both here and in other poems, have sometimes been dismissed as whimsical trivialities that add nothing to the reader's experience.

In fact, Apollinaire took these innovations very seriously and was fascinated both by literary form and by the typographic revolution that was taking place in the early twentieth century.[34] He began to develop his picture poems during the period of intense creativity in the arts just before the war when he may have felt in danger of being left behind. They represented a move on his part towards finding new poetic energy and forms, in part inspired by the abstraction he was seeing in the visual arts, although Apollinaire never fully abandoned his lyric voice or wished to follow groups such as the futurists in their pursuit of violence and speed.[35]

We can only speculate about how Lou reacted to these poems. Her suitor's decision to join up clearly shocked her, however. The '*paradis artificiel*' of Apollinaire's life in Nice was at an end, and the scene was set for both the poet's introduction to military life and a sudden intensification of his relationship with Lou.

To LOU DE COLIGNY-CHÂTILLON HOMAGE

respectfully passionate

O li
ve tre
es you f
lutt ered
to die to just as
and at her eye
know ir lash es s
last ome times
res ist do Through this book hard
ible E and precise in its joy
ter ni
ty

Your hair like I lear n o Lou to know me
spilt blood SALUT so as never again to forget me
E YO
U LOU but per
AS YO che d on
UR F th e ab
AVOU yss I d
RITE om ina
TREE D te the
OES IN sea li
THE LA ke a
RGE MA mas ter
RATIM
E GARD
EN RAI
SED UP L
IKE A B
REAST

and I pla ce her

e des pite you

y
o
u r m o s t
secret thoughts

Guillaume

Apollin aire

2
NÎMES
DECEMBER 1914–APRIL 1915
(SOLDIERING)

Although British and Belgian troops were involved in the conflict from August 1914 onwards it was the French Army that bore the brunt of the German offensive in the early months of the war, and by the end of the year it had experienced very mixed fortunes. It had launched an early attack into Alsace-Lorraine that proved abortive. It had then endured a long, hard retreat and faced potential catastrophe as the right wing of the German advance swept through Belgium and deep into French territory. Rallying in front of Paris in what became known as the Miracle of the Marne, with the support of its allies the French Army had forced the Germans to retreat to defensive positions on the Aisne river and its tributaries, stabilizing the front along a line that would remain largely intact for much of the rest of the war.[1] Above all, the army had held firm and prevented the Germans from repeating their quick victories of 1870.

All this came at enormous cost. As Hew Strachan points out, the casualties for the belligerent armies during 1914 were the highest of the entire war in relation to their establishments.[2] The total French dead for the first five months of the conflict has been estimated at 265,000, but casualties of all types, including wounded and missing, had already reached 385,000 by 10 September. On 22 August alone 27,000 died. Moreover, a significant portion of northern France remained under occupation at the end of the year, including the *départements* that contained much of the country's manufacturing industry and most of its coal and iron-ore resources.[3] This would be no short war.

Apollinaire could not remain untouched by the course of events, despite his infatuation with his new muse. Friends and colleagues were involved in a titanic struggle while he was taking day trips to local beauty spots.[4] A letter to Lou on 29 November suggests that he was keenly affected by reports from the front: 'In it [the newspaper *Le Petit Niçois*] I read a marvellous military account, the story of the battle of the Ourcq that saved Paris and was an important phase in the battle of the Marne.' Frustration with his lack of success with Lou was no doubt a major factor in his decision to renew his application to enlist, but a sense of duty also played its part. As he told the writer and critic Paul Léautaud at Christmas 1914, 'I spent four months in Nice which were the delights of Capua . . . In the end I had to tear myself away from this happiness in order to do my duty. I didn't have the right to act in any other way.'[5]

Given the military situation (Borie's connections must also have helped), things moved quickly. Having sought the commandant's support in late November Apollinaire went in front of a medical board on 4 December 1914, at the same time renewing his request for naturalization. On the following day he enlisted for the duration of the war and early on the morning of Sunday 6 December he left Nice to join the 38th Field Artillery Regiment in Nîmes.[6] Despite his age (at thirty-four he was almost twice as old as some of his new comrades), he was almost certain to see active service – another consequence of the carnage in the early months of the war.[7]

Heavy artillery barrages 'softening up' enemy positions before attacking troops 'go over the top' have become one of the defining images of the Great War. But the armies of all the major combatants entered the conflict expecting a campaign of manoeuvre. Heavy guns, which commanders viewed primarily as siege weapons, made up a much smaller proportion of the overall mix than they would do later in the war after it had become clear that an infantry offensive was almost certain to fail without the support of powerful artillery.[8]

The French Army in particular, with its traditional stress on taking the offensive, had built its artillery arm around the light field gun, deployed in small groups, or batteries, that were designed to provide close mobile support to the infantry over open sights rather than to deliver crushing preliminary bombardments in preparation for an attack.[9] In April 1914, therefore, there were only fifty-eight batteries of heavy artillery in mainland France as opposed to 618 field artillery and thirty horse artillery batteries.[10]

The mainstay of the French light field artillery regiments was the famous 75-millimetre gun, or *soixante-quinze*, officially designated the Matériel de 75mm Mle 1897. On its introduction in the late 1890s it had turned the artillery world upside down, rendering all existing field guns obsolete through its novel combination of features such as fixed ammunition, quick-acting breech mechanism and on-carriage recoil system (the design of which was treated as a state secret), all of which allowed the crew to achieve fire rates of up to twenty aimed rounds per minute.[11] Although the gun's limitations against entrenched positions, in particular its low trajectory and the small weight of its shell, would rapidly become apparent, it remained in widespread use throughout the war. Seventeen thousand had been produced by 1918.[12]

A 75-millimetre battery had four guns, each of which was served by a large complement of men and horses – the armies of 1914 remained almost Napoleonic in their dependence on animal power. Typically, one team of six horses, arranged in pairs, pulled the gun and a small limber carrying ammunition and stores, while a second team of six horses pulled two more limbers. The horses were controlled by six drivers, or *conducteurs*, who rode the left-hand animal of each pair. The gun itself had six gunners (*servants*) three to handle the ammunition and three to deal with the aiming and firing. In addition, a senior non-commissioned officer (typically a sergeant or *maréchal des logis*) acted as gun captain (*chef de pièce*), supported by a corporal (*brigadier*), who was responsible for the harnessing and for linking with the rest of the battery's guns, some of which might be in firing positions while others were in rear areas. A range of other men served the battery as a whole, including a battery commander, an observer and a telephonist. At one time or another Apollinaire was to carry out several of these roles.

Life in the artillery was no soft option. Apart from the normal activities of military life, such as sentry duty, the artilleryman could expect to spend a lot of time travelling over rough ground, either in the saddle or seated on limbers, as well as physically man-handling the guns into position.[13] The battery's large team of horses needed constant attention – 'I'm not used to these stable-boy duties', Apollinaire complained to his friends the Mortiers[14] – while gun-laying required serious mathematical ability. And the close support role given to the field artillery in French military thinking, which necessitated constant contact with the front-line infantry, often brought artillerymen within easy range of enemy guns or even machine-gun fire.[15] In Jacques Meyer's view the 75-millimetre gunner was therefore the combatant who was most like the front-line infantryman.[16]

In his very first letter to Lou after joining his regiment, sent on 10 December, Apollinaire made the rigours of his new life immediately apparent. 'This morning, got up in the dark, roll call in the rain . . . At half past six they show me how to saddle up in the stable.' Just a few days later, on the 16th, there was an 'excursion on impossible roads in the middle of cannon fire because they were using live ammunition'. The following day brought horse-riding followed by grooming, exposure to live firing, a fourteen-kilometre march and gun drill. And so continued what Apollinaire called his 'weekly routine, trotting, polishing, theory, drill, gunnery'.

Perhaps not surprisingly, the letters to Lou were punctuated by complaints about minor illnesses. In mid-December Apollinaire mentioned stomach upsets, which were made worse by the cold weather. During much of January 1915 he was in the grip of a bad cold. More worryingly, in late December there was an outbreak of scarlet fever in the barracks, fortunately not affecting his block. The intense winter cold only served to highlight deficiencies in the standard equipment issued to the recruits. Apollinaire's stomach ache began to improve when he improvised a flannel belt for his midriff.

Working with horses also had its dangers, particularly as many of the animals were former cart horses unused to military work or had been imported in a semi-broken state from as far away as Canada or Argentina. A horse stepped on Apollinaire's foot on 20 December – 'I saw stars' – but luckily there was no break. Falls remained a constant concern, particularly as the training often took place over rough and frozen ground and involved dangerous exercises, such as lying with one's face towards the rear end of the horse, arms and legs hanging loose. On the morning of 22 December he took a tumble. 'I was thrown forward on to my side. All my bones creaked, my back ached and I got up quickly to avoid being kicked.' A few hours later he had a further fall, again without damage. Others were not so lucky. Three days after Christmas his colleague Combet was kicked in the leg by a horse and required an operation to remove many bone fragments. In January 1915 another comrade smashed his head at the gallop against a wall (he survived but in February was invalided out of the army).

Barrack-room life – which Apollinaire describes as 'violent monotony' – brought its own degradations. A letter on 18 December, for instance, describes a freezing night-time sentry duty aimed at preventing the recruits from urinating inside. 'You can imagine how sad it was,' he wrote. 'All alone in the corridors of the barracks in the most terrible cold.' Other anecdotes illustrate what the poet perceives as 'the brutishness inherent in barrack life'. On Christmas Day Apollinaire found a chaffinch dead from the cold but still warm. He wanted to try to revive it, but a senior officer ordered him to take it to the mess so that it could be eaten.

The way in which the army operated made things worse. Unexplained decisions created a perpetual air of uncertainty and left the barracks awash with rumours. As Apollinaire said in his letter to Lou on Christmas Day 1914, 'The maxim here is: "*There's no point trying to understand.*"' Departures for the front were organized in a rapid and brutal way. 'Leaving doesn't take long. The men are designated in the evening, they leave the following morning . . . They no longer allow us to approach those we know to say goodbye.' Discipline, too, was often harsh. Failing to manage a horse properly could lead to a week's detention. An encounter with one soldier under guard left the poet shaken. 'He told me he'd remember the gunners and if he met soldiers from the 38th at the front it wouldn't be the Prussians he'd be firing at.'

Understandably, the recruits became obsessed with the arrival of letters and the possibilities for leave. But mail was delivered intermittently and out of sequence, fostering misunderstandings and concerns that the common practice of numbering correspondence did little to alleviate.[17] 'My treasure,' Apollinaire wrote to Lou on Christmas Day 1914, 'forgive the sadness in my last letters. I didn't receive anything from you! . . . Today I've received your letters VIII and X. I don't have IX'. Meanwhile, leave at this stage in the war was a privilege not a right for French soldiers, and its granting was capricious and grudging. Permission to depart was often confirmed only at the last minute, and a large part of any period of leave could easily be consumed in travelling. As Apollinaire explained in a letter to Lou on 23 December, 'I'm almost certain that I won't have leave for the New Year. The fault lies with the railway companies. Ordinary soldiers no longer have the right to take an express train. In current conditions you need 38 hours to travel from Nîmes to Nice by slow train.' (The same journey today takes around four hours.) In the event, the poet was able to spend New Year with Lou in Nice but only after much uncertainty.[18]

Underlying all the letters from the early period of the poet's entry into army life is a moving sense of isolation, despite the constant round of activity.[19] 'Yesterday evening in bed,' he wrote on 29 December, 'I really felt that close proximity to others where you are always alone, that isolation where you can never really be on your own – that's barracks for you.' On Christmas Day he was awoken in a way that illustrates unforgettably this loneliness within the crowd. 'This morning towards 5 a.m. before roll call I woke up to the creaking of beds that were squeaking in rhythm. Most of my comrades in the dormitory were wanking.'

In early 1915 Apollinaire's status changed in a way that both relieved and exacerbated the pressures on him: he left the group of trainee non-commissioned officers to which he had been assigned on 16 December in order to join a team of trainee reserve officers (*élèves officiers de réserve* or ÉOR). At first he hoped to bypass the normal entry procedures. 'Given my reputation in civilian life I got in without an examination or competition on the decision of the captain commanding the depot.'[20] But his letter to Lou on 5 January 1915 announcing the news suggested that there had been an almighty row as a result. Four days later he began sitting the entry examinations after all, leaving him little time to prepare.

The poet's letters during this short period offer a fascinating insight into the literary and scientific skills required of aspiring artillery officers in the French Army and the barriers to promotion for those who did not possess them. The first examination was French composition on the topic of 'The physical and chemical properties of the atmosphere' followed by a history paper on the wars in the reign of Louis XV. On the following day (Sunday 10 January) came mathematics – arithmetic, algebra and geometry: 'all things that, like any self-respecting poet, I know nothing about'.[21] The tests concluded on the Monday with artillery, voice projection and leadership. Despite his dismissive comments Apollinaire felt he had done well and was encouraged by his colonel, who called him into his office where a richly comic scene unfolded. 'Then he cited the poets who have been soldiers; however, he only found André Chénier, who, all things considered, was never a soldier. All this time in his office I was standing to attention with my carbine, chin strap in place.'

When the results were announced Apollinaire had indeed been classed first for French style and composition but had also proved one of the strongest candidates in artillery. His friend Nicolini had come first in the sciences. They would henceforth be part of a group of older, more mature men who would move through the ranks of corporal and sergeant, becoming second lieutenants in the reserve after three months of satisfactory progress.

Others had their shortcomings brutally pointed out by the army hierarchy. 'Only one of those from the 2nd Mountain Regiment from Nice had been taken, the others were really disappointed. They told me that their service as gunners on foot with their packs and marches in the mountains was very hard and they'd hoped to better their lot. The colonel told them they'd all been as useless as each other and they were only taking one so they didn't entirely give up hope, and the one who'd been picked could count himself lucky because he'd been chosen by lot.' Clearly, practical experience and questions of morale counted for little.

Becoming a trainee officer brought immediate practical advantages, as Apollinaire's letter to Lou on 12 January 1915 makes clear. 'A soldier makes my bed, no more parade . . . no more grooming, sweeping and peeling potatoes.' The poet now shared accommodation with just three other colleagues, and discipline was much more relaxed: 'We do what we want, put on the lights when we want.' He foresaw more opportunities for leave and to stay overnight in Nîmes itself rather than in the barracks.

However, it quickly became apparent that joining the ÉOR was a Faustian pact. For a start, Apollinaire's workload increased dramatically immediately after his incorporation into the group. His letter to Lou on 5 January sets out the new regime. 'The workload is becoming fantastic. I've three hours of horse-riding every day. Here's what I've done today when I started as an ÉOR. 7.30 till 9 riding, trotting, exercises on horseback, rubbing down until 9.15, 9.15 till 10 o'clock artillery theory – (difficult), 10 till 11 lunch, polishing, 11 till midday classroom training, midday till 2 o'clock riding, trotting and galloping, 2 till 3.30 practical artillery, 4 till 4.30 drill.'[22] He had to study in the evening and by 8 January he was admitting to being 'a little perturbed and maddened by the large number of new things we have to learn at the same time and God knows there are enough of them'.

The situation improved little with time; indeed there was a growing feeling that the army was pushing Apollinaire and his fellow trainees too hard, as a letter to Lou dated 21 January testifies. 'But I've had it up to here with all their geometry, algebra, horse-riding, artillery and all the other rubbish. They're taking advantage . . . on the pretext that we need to get there quickly they're going too far.' The sense of exhaustion continued to increase during early February when the rigorous training was clearly beginning to take its physical toll on the recruits. 'They make us do jumps, stupid things in the Nîmes countryside which is like a skeleton . . . Nothing but sharp stones like bare bones. Accidents every day . . . I'm tired, I can't bring my knees together any longer.' On 4 February he announced to Lou that he had taken the decision to leave the group if the authorities continued to 'mess me about too much'.

A further consequence of joining the ÉOR was that the poet's move to the front was deferred by several months. In some ways this suited Apollinaire in his relationship with Lou, but he clearly found his lack of direct engagement in the conflict frustrating, almost cowardly, particularly as a major spring offensive was expected. 'I'm ashamed sometimes of my happiness and my inaction far from the war . . . There are times . . . when I would ask to be moved into the infantry in order to leave more quickly. I find there are too many people in our depots. Above all, too many cowards,' he admitted on 28 January. One can see these concerns reflected in the rather bloodthirsty content and overblown patriotism of the poem 'Dans un café à Nîmes' ('In a Café in Nîmes') that Apollinaire sent to Lou on 4 February 1915. The final three stanzas read:

> Corporal going off to the trenches
> How happy your glorious fate
> There in the gouged-out lines
> From your imperious rifles
> Victories will be hung

In a depot we the gunners
Await our turn for glory
You were the first to leave
We will win the victory
That crowns the last arrivals –

Gunner have patience
Farewell then – Farewell corporal –
Your name – My name Hope
I am a cannon a horse
I am Hope Vive la France[23]

Apollinaire's disillusionment was to be further exacerbated by a bombshell from on high. He had already realized how difficult it was to become an officer in the artillery, but in early February he heard rumours of a ministerial decision that would restrict formal promotion to junior-officer positions to soldiers actually serving at the front. There was further clarification at the end of month. 'A new ministerial circular forbids promotion in the depots, so we'll leave as soon as our training's finished as drivers (first class), and we'll only get promotion at the front once we've proved ourselves.' During February and March it is clear from his letters that Apollinaire was mulling over the implications of this change of policy and, in particular, whether he would be better going to the front immediately as a private soldier and seeking promotion in the field.[24] Certainly it must have made the prospect of yet more studying even less attractive.

It would be a mistake, however, to imagine that Apollinaire was constantly depressed during late 1914 and early 1915. Military service had its disadvantages, and the poet's relationship with Lou continued to be turbulent, but the letters portray a man who remained keenly interested in events, the literary world and what he called the 'opera' of life around him.[25]

He followed the progress of the war closely, reading French, Italian and even Austrian newspapers, and his judgements were often shrewd. He noted on 20 December, for instance, that the French authorities had allowed the Garibaldi Legion, made up of Italian volunteers, only to make a token contribution to the fighting because 'they don't want an Italy that can't make up its mind to be able to say that lots of its nationals died in the service of France'. From the outset he was fully aware of the human consequences of the conflict. The French Army would prevail, but at what cost? 'It's our destiny to live through such catastrophes,' he wrote in the same letter on 20 December. Nor did he have any illusions that the war would end quickly. At the end of 1914 he predicted at least a further year of fighting and continued political disruption for the decade to come. 'We're in a warlike time. I think it will last even longer than people are saying, and we won't perhaps see real peace before 1930.' By February 1915 his estimate had increased to two years, but he believed (correctly) that a long war would not suit the Germans. He makes an extended comparison between the current period and the Middle Ages, branding the times he was living through 'the time of Anguish'.

In their appraisal of France's allies the letters perhaps reflect the wider prejudices of the French military. News that German ships had bombarded the English coast in December 1914 prompted an outburst of contempt. 'Those damn English are really degenerate sailors. The Germans bombard their ports at will, it's disgusting.' By January 1915, when he had a conversation with an old schoolfriend, now working as an interpreter with the British Army, the poet's views had obviously softened (he had by then seen British officers and their Indian troops in Marseilles), but the portrait of well-dressed but ineffective soldiers was hardly convincing. 'He gave me a good insight into the English, very chic, very comfortable, mediocre soldiers, Hindus, too, except the Gurkhas, who are very good soldiers.'

However, Apollinaire was equally, if not more, critical of some of his compatriots, above all those recruited from southern France, demonstrating a prejudice that seems to have been widespread in the army. On 30 December he wrote to Lou that the soldiers from Nice were hardly fanatical supporters of the war but they were not cowards, unlike their comrades from Marseilles who were 'poems of pusillanimity'.[26] The letters also vividly illustrate a major reason for this lack of enthusiasm: the war was eating up men, for many of whom the north of France was like a separate country.[27] Noting that six hundred men were leaving the Nîmes depot for the front, Apollinaire admitted to Lou in late January that 'it seems that the 38th is one of the artillery reg'ts. most badly hit, particularly as regards officers'. Morale in some of the colonial units was especially bad, as a conversation with a medical officer serving with a Senegalese regiment confirmed. 'He told me that it was complete butchery, and the officer corps in the Senegalese regiment entirely sacrificed, the doctor at 300 metres from the front because the officers know that their men won't pick them up and they want to feel the doctors close by them.'

Meanwhile, literary life continued. Apollinaire's belief in the crucial role of the poet remained unshaken. 'The profession of poet is neither useless, nor mad, nor frivolous,' he told Lou. 'Poets are the creators . . . Nothing then appears on earth, becomes apparent to mankind if it hasn't first been imagined by a poet.' The period in Nice had proved relatively unproductive, but from Nîmes he began to send poems to Lou with increasing frequency, sometimes embedded in his letters, sometimes as separate sheets. He was clearly still thinking hard about his poetic practice and told his friend Jean Mollet in mid-January 1915 that he had found new 'more startling and much more complicated' methods.[28] At the same time he kept up with literary gossip and corresponded with other authors, including figures such as Remy de Gourmont, whom he believed to be one of the best, if not the best, French writer of the time.

The letters are full of amusing stories and anecdotes narrated with relish. The whole regiment has its genitals inspected in what the soldiers dub *la revue des queues* (a pricks' parade). A Polish cubist painter is arrested on suspicion of spying because his drawings are taken to be maps.[29] A cold-infested woman travelling by train uses four handkerchiefs in sequence and then carefully lays them out to dry in the compartment she shares with the other voyagers. Apollinaire had always enjoyed gathering and displaying arcane pieces of knowledge – his early poetry is shot through with obscure references – and army life opened new horizons or brought back memories from his extensive reading. In a letter to Lou on 30 January 1915 he mused on soldiers' slang. '*Le Pastisse*, this word applies to everything that's a bit mixed up. War is *le pastisse* . . . all our work is *le pastisse*, the word comes from the Nissard dialect.' Even artillery training, despite its rigours, appealed to the autodidact in him. Mathematics proved more fascinating than he had expected – 'I would never have thought I would have the courage to learn such strange things,' he wrote on 19 January 1915 – while he took pleasure in the practical aspects of being a gunner.

In fact, the letters to Lou during Apollinaire's time in Nîmes demonstrate a real pride in his emerging competence as well as a growing ambition for promotion.[30] Within two weeks of signing up, he felt able to write, 'I rub down and massage my horse as if I'd done this all my life', adding three days later that he was no longer a raw recruit. In early January 1915 he had his first taste of command, which seemed to go well. When Lou was preparing to visit Toutou, a serving artilleryman, in early February 1915, Apollinaire was keen to underline his newfound professionalism. 'Tell him that I handle mils and decigrades very skilfully and I'm soon going to take command of my first salvo . . . Ask him as well whether they often use the offset ranging (on the 75) at the front.' Overall, then, life was not so bad, and even in his descriptions of the toughest of times Apollinaire is likely to remark that it had been a 'good day' or that he had had 'a fine excursion'.

Alongside competence came unexpected comradeship. The letters mention singing and philosophical discussions, while barrack-room pranks built an *esprit de corps*, as well as illustrating the immense fatigue and the rough humour induced by military life. 'The mail sergeant in dormitory 69, Giraud, a baritone at the Opéra Comique, gathered us together to watch the dormitory's storekeeper as he slept. He was sleeping like an angel, his bonnet on his head, a cigarette on his lips, we made a racket, the baritone sang, we used a lighter to light his cigarette, we tied him to his bed, finally using a match we set light to his moustache, he sat up in bed his face on fire, broke the cords and fell back on his left side snoring. It was an extraordinarily comic and amusing scene.' A poem sent to Lou on Christmas Day 1914 captures this growing sense of belonging:

> The smoke in the mess is like the coming night
> Voices high or deep and wine bleeds everywhere
> I draw on my pipe proud and free among my comrades
> They will leave with me for the battlefields
> They will sleep at night in the rain or under the stars
> They will gallop with me with victories riding pillion
> They will obey the same orders as I will
> They will listen carefully to the sublime trumpet calls

They will die near me and perhaps I will die near them
They will suffer from the cold and the heat with me
They are true men these ones who drink with me
They obey like me the laws of the male
They watch on their marches the women passing by
They lust after them but my love is on a higher plane
A love that rules my heart my senses and my brain
And which is my homeland my family and my hope
For me a soldier in love a soldier of sweet France[31]

We need to remember, however, that Apollinaire's experience at this stage of his military career was not necessarily typical of all recruits. If his age and previous career as a writer made the physical hardships of army life more apparent (learning to ride at thirty-four was particularly difficult, he told Laure Faure-Favier), they also offered significant advantages. For a start he was never short of correspondence, on one memorable day – Christmas Eve 1914 – receiving forty-two letters: 'It seems that I've beaten the record of all the regiments stationed in Nîmes, where there are 17,000 men at the moment.' He also had an established network of personal connections that he exploited shamelessly both to help Lou and for his own benefit. On 16 January 1915, for instance, he told Lou, 'I'd written to Borys about my leave and also about the group of trainee officers.[32] He's written to the colonel and captain today. It's too late for the ÉOR group, but I hope that now Borys is involved it might influence the final examination.'

It is clear also that his status as a poet makes Apollinaire something of a celebrity, both among his comrades, for whom he writes verses that they can send to their sweethearts, and with his senior officers.[33] His colonel, for one, seems quite awe-struck if the letters are to be believed. 'Thus, he told me, in front of all the soldiers, I've had the pleasure of coming to appreciate your mind, your education, and you've given me the subtle satisfaction of talking about poetry with you.' Even if there is some exaggeration for Lou's benefit (she later admitted she had little idea of Apollinaire's literary status), the prestige attached to a published author in France was considerable.[34]

Overall then the letters give a rich and nuanced picture of Apollinaire's months in training. But by late March 1915 the pressure for change was building, not just as a result of the poet's increasing impatience to get to the front but because of emotional factors. His relationship with Lou had reached a crisis point.

3
NÎMES
DECEMBER 1914–APRIL 1915
(LOU)

If Apollinaire intended to provoke Lou into action by his enlistment and sudden departure from Nice he succeeded beyond all expectations. In an act that perhaps symbolizes her love of the spontaneous and unexpected as much as any great passion for the poet, she arrived the next day outside Apollinaire's barracks in Nîmes, and for the following nine nights, until her return to Saint-Jean-Cap-Ferrat on 16 December, she stayed at the Grand Hôtel du Midi et de la Poste. During this time the new recruit spent every moment he could spare from his duties with her. Three later periods of leave reunited the couple – in Nice over New Year 1914–15 and between 23 and 25 January 1915 and in Marseille on 28 March 1915 – before Apollinaire's departure for the front in early April.

Their meetings were intensely sexual. There are strong hints in Apollinaire's letters that he and Lou had been physically intimate during the previous autumn in Nice. On 1 December the poet referred to his 'foretaste' of Lou's flesh and on the 18th to 'those tender arguments in Saint-Jean . . . after which our reconciliation was so exquisite'. Apollinaire had certainly not been short of women companions in the past. His first great poem, 'La Chanson du mal-aimé' ('The Song of the Ill-Loved One'), had been inspired by a possibly unconsummated infatuation with a young Englishwoman, Annie Playden, in the early 1900s; his later affair with the painter Marie Laurencin was also a fruitful source of poetry. Meanwhile, there seem to have been many casual liaisons

– indeed Apollinaire told Lou that his friend and self-styled 'secretary' Jean Mollet had written to express his surprise that 'the delicate butterfly should have come to rest on a flower and no longer moves. Certainly something has changed in the machine.' None the less, Lou's visit to Nîmes in early December unleashed an unprecedented flood of erotic fantasy and practice, doubtless intensified by the loneliness and exhaustion of the poet's regime in his barracks.

The poet's letters to Lou between mid-December 1914 and early April 1915 describe an arc that can roughly be divided into four sections. The early part of Apollinaire's correspondence, to the end of 1914, radiates a contentment that the relationship had moved on to a new level combined with an increasingly extravagant idealization of Lou's qualities. On 10 December, for instance, while she was still in Nîmes, Apollinaire told her, 'I think of you, of your adorable body, of your dear soul, so simple and so profound.' Lou writes marvellously, she is a model of grace and goodness, the whole universe is contained within her, the poet affirms. By 23 December Lou had become 'my goddess, my mythology, my fable'; on Christmas Day she was 'my music, my poetry, my nine Muses, my three Graces'. She was his one true love, and the two other women he thought he had loved before no longer existed. The love between the poet and his muse was like 'a great bird that would fly higher than aeroplanes, it climbs unceasingly, an angelic bird, into the sublime regions of the ether'.

At the same time the poet's success in conquering Lou in the battle of love is explicitly linked to his destiny as a soldier – he speaks of 'glory itself, which calls us and which is represented for me by my complete and definitive possession of you'. She is the only thing it is worth being a soldier to defend. A poem sent to Lou on 17 December reinforced the connection through a series of images that intermingled military life with Lou's qualities:

I think of you my Lou your heart is my barracks
My senses are your horses your memory is my lucerne

The sky is full tonight of sabres and spurs
The gunners depart heavy and prompt in the dark

But near me incessantly I see your image
Your mouth is the burning wound of courage

Our trumpet blasts burst in the night like your voice
When I am on horseback you trot near me

Our 75s are graceful like your body
And your hair is tawny like the fire of a shell exploding in the north

I love you your hands and my memories
Cause a constant happy fanfare to sound
Suns begin to neigh turn by turn
We are the stable partitions against which the stars kick[1]

By the end of 1914, then, Apollinaire was hoping that their love would be 'the most beautiful and the most complete that has ever been experienced under the heavens'.

Meanwhile, as their New Year meeting approached, the correspondence became ever more erotically charged and direct. Apollinaire's letter on 18 December still used very traditional and coy poetic language to refer to 'our embraces . . . our wild kisses . . . our tremblings . . . our tender feelings'. By 23 December the poet was signing off his letter, 'If you knew how much I want you!!!' On Christmas Day he received two letters from Lou, in one of which she described a night of masturbation, prompting an immediate and unbridled response from Apollinaire. 'I adore you my darling. I desire you. I penetrate you with my member up to the hilt. I've an erection like Nimrod's bow.' Three days later, he told her crudely, 'At the moment, I want you enough to burst the flies on my artilleryman's trousers.' However, these bald statements of the poet's desire are often balanced by poems of some delicacy, as the following extract suggests:

> My Lou night is falling you're mine I love you
> The cypresses have grown dark so too the sky
> The bugles sang your beauty and my content
> At loving you for ever your heart near my heart
> I have come back gently to the barracks
> The stables smelled good the lucerne
> The croupes of the horses evoked your strength and grace
> A golden chestnut mare oh my beautiful thoroughbred
> The Magne Tower revolved on its laurel-crowned hill
> And danced slowly slowly filled with shadows
> While lovers came down from the hill
> The tower danced slowly like a Saracen girl
> The wind is blowing but it's not at all cold
> I shall see you in two days and I'm happy as a king[2]

After much uncertainty Apollinaire was given leave to spend two days with Lou in Nice over New Year and later sent a description of the hectic round of socializing and sex to his friend Jean Mollet.

The poet's letters between this meeting and Lou's departure for the Argonne in early February 1915 (the second section of our arc) are even more intense than before. Alongside passages of real tenderness ('O Lou my beloved, I bless you for having given me an extraordinary love affair') there are moments where the poet continues to idealize their relationship or indulges in high-flown rhetoric, as when he describes Lou's breasts as being 'like meringues on which a pink sunset had snowed'. But the overall tone is darker, more sexually explicit and demanding, as if Apollinaire the pornographer and editor of de Sade and other writers of erotica now had the upper hand over Apollinaire the troubadour and lyric poet.[3]

On 2 January 1915 he talks of 'the parts I whipped that writhed so carnally those final nights'. Three days later there are references to anal sex. 'I take you completely and everywhere at the same time, even where it makes you so afraid and causes you such pain.' Even allowing for a large element of erotic fantasy and the playing out of master–slave roles there is a new undertone of violence and sadism in the letters of this period. 'It's your buttocks I want to horsewhip,' Apollinaire wrote on 8 January. 'I'll whip them until they become bloody until they look like a mix of raspberries and cream.' A letter sent on 11 January contains another fantasy in which he would have 'trampled on your belly and your behind one after the other with my artilleryman's hob-nailed boots. And once you were covered in bruises I would have impaled you.'

During February Lou would reproach Apollinaire for having developed a taste for vice in her to which the poet responded with a passionate defence of the freedom of the imagination and the senses in a poem entitled 'Parce que tu m'as parlé de vice . . .' ('Because You Spoke to Me of Vice . . .'):

> You spoke to me of vice in yesterday's letter
> Vice has no place in sublime love affairs
> It is no more than a grain of sand in the sea
> A solitary grain sinking into the murky abyss
>
> We can put our imagination into play
> Make our senses dance on the wreckage of the world
> Exhaust ourselves to the point of exasperation
> Or wallow together in a foul mire

And bound one to another in a unique embrace
We can defy death and its destiny
When our teeth will chatter in chattering panic
We can call evening what others call morning

You can make a god of my savage will
I can prostrate myself as at an altar
Before your buttocks bloodied by my frenzy
Our love will remain pure like a beautiful sky

What does it matter if breathless silent open-mouthed
Like two cannons fallen from their carriages
Broken by too much loving our bodies lie inert
Our love will always remain what it was

Let us ennoble the imagination my heart
Poor humanity often has so little of it
Vice in all this is only an illusion
That only ever deceives vulgar souls[4]

The newfound carnality in their relationship after Apollinaire's
enlistment did not bring the poet unalloyed joy, however. Within
two weeks of leaving Nice his separation from Lou had already
become a form of torture. 'I feel more and more how cruel it is to
be separated from you. I'm sad this evening, dear Lou, darkly sad,'
he wrote on 21 December. Despite being well aware of the vagaries
of the post he became increasingly anxious – indeed furious – at
any gap in Lou's correspondence with him. He had received forty-
two letters in one day, he claimed on 24 December, 'but among
those 42 letters not one from Lou, Lou forgets me . . . Write to
me, I adore you, but I'm furious. Write to me, Lou!' Following the
arrival of two letters on Christmas Day he acknowledges that he

has been 'stupidly jealous' and that he is 'a great animal when he has doubts or becomes enraged'.

After their meeting at New Year Apollinaire's feelings deepened – he loved her a thousand times more than before, he stated, and 'with more seriousness than ever' – but so, too, did his anxiety. On 3 January 1915 he was 'sad about the praise you gave to your previous lovers. I wonder how someone like me, who doesn't have any great physical attractions, can compete with the memory of such handsome young men.' On the following day he expressed his concern that she had begun to love him less, a concern that began to surface ever more frequently.

During January and early February Apollinaire's moods became worse and his letters more gloomy, no doubt reflecting, at least in part, the physical exhaustion caused by his trainee-officer role as well as his emotional state. When he feels that Lou is preoccupied with other things and not reading his correspondence with enough care he heads a letter with the instruction 'A letter to read in its entirety!!!' She was enjoying herself in Nice and flirting with strangers, he claimed, while he suffered in Nîmes. He tells her off for being a 'little snob' and for 'such ridiculous carryings-on'. That she was clearly beginning to express reservations about their affair made him alternately angry and cajoling. The time that the couple spent together in Nice between 23 and 25 January did little to relieve the poet's increasing unhappiness. Written on the 30th, the poem 'Si je mourais là-bas' ('If I Were to Die Out There'), quoted earlier, gives a revealing insight into Apollinaire's feelings at this point, with its reminder of his potential fate at the front, its underlying concern about being forgotten, its ambivalent declarations of love and obsession and its implicit threat that he will come back to haunt her.

*

On 6 February 1915 Lou set out on a difficult and potentially hazardous trip to visit her long-standing male friend Toutou on the Argonne front, where he was serving as a sergeant in the artillery. Getting permission to travel to a war zone had involved an immense amount of effort and string-pulling, to which Apollinaire had lent his support, although in the end her pass was obtained through her own contacts in Nice. Lou's stay would last until well into March and marked a turning point in her relationship with the poet.

In practical terms her departure made their correspondence more difficult to sustain, and by 12 February Apollinaire was already very agitated about the lack of contact. 'My dearest heart, write to me, write to me. I don't know why you don't write to me. Write . . . does Lou forget me? It's maddening how anxious you can get.' The first stanza of a poem included in the same letter expresses his concern in apocalyptic terms:

> Four days oh my love and no letter from you
> The day is no more the sun has been drowned
> The barracks have become a house of horror
> And I am as sad as a transported horse[5]

But her trip also finally brought home to Apollinaire that he was never going to be at the centre of Lou's life in the way he had hoped – she had, after all, resisted all attempts since her initial visit in December to make a similar trip to Nîmes despite constant encouragement from Apollinaire. Toutou was always going to come first, and Apollinaire would remain at best the fifth wheel on Lou's car, as he put it memorably in a letter on 17 March. The letters during this third section in the arc of their relationship therefore combine moments of intense and unremitting anguish (particularly when Apollinaire dwelt on the dangers Lou faced at the front) with an increasingly fatalistic acceptance that their affair was drawing to a close.

Where once Lou could expect to receive a daily letter and often more – three letters and two poems from 3 February exist – the flow now seemed to reduce significantly, although it is possible that some of the correspondence may have been lost. There are letters or poems dated 6, 7, 8, 9, 10 and 12 February but then a gap until the 23rd. A short note on the 26th and a longer letter on the 27th are only followed up by a letter on 6 March and a poem on 11 March. And so it continued until the daily rhythm picked up once again towards the end of that month.

The content of the letters began to change, too. There are more frequent references to his possible departure for the front and to the likelihood of their having to say goodbye. In late February Apollinaire wrote that: 'from 7 March they will be able to make me leave when they want, only letting me know the evening before for the following morning. So I wish you *au revoir*, my dear friend, unless it's *adieu*.' He began to talk about Lou in the past tense – 'you had become my joy, my hope, my courage . . . and you would have played an important role in the history of literature'. He was now bending his will to breaking his love for her. A poem entitled 'Faction' ('Guard Duty') sent on 25 March reflects his continuing feelings for her, his suffering and the melancholy passage of lived experience into memory:

> I'm thinking of you my Lou during guard duty
> I see your eyes up there in the blinking of stars
> All the sky is your body a precious creation
> Of my keen desire which is fanned by the gusts
> Around this soldier in meditation

Love you know nothing of what absence means
And you know not how one feels like dying
Every hour adds infinitely to the suffering
And when the day ends you begin to suffer
And when night returns the pain begins anew

I place my hopes in Memory o my Love
It rejuvenates it embellishes when it fades
You will grow old Love you'll grow old one day
Memory in the distance sounds a hunting horn
O slow slow night o my rifle so heavy[6]

However, there was to be one final meeting in the south of France, at the Hotel Terminus in Marseilles on 28 March, an encounter that Apollinaire would describe as strange and very pleasant. As well as renewing their sexual relations the couple seem to have come to some sort of agreement: on his part to calm down and to accept Lou's independence (and, by implication, the pre-eminence of Toutou in her emotional life); on hers to be more honest about her activities and feelings and to make more effort to keep in regular contact. The lovers were to become friends. 'That would be even more amazing, doing and saying everything, being gods!' Apollinaire wrote on the April, making, it would seem, the best of a bad job.

The frequency of Apollinaire's letters picked up once again during the short period before his transfer to northern France and the front (the fourth and final section of the arc), and their tone was indeed less feverish, with the poet reassuring Lou that 'my depression and my irritability in Marseilles quickly disappeared'. Perhaps as a way of demonstrating his acceptance of the change in their relationship Apollinaire began to talk about a young woman of good family he had now met in Nîmes and who seemed set to become Lou's 'replacement' (fidelity clearly not being part of the agreement with Lou). More significantly, having asked Lou on a number of occasions to keep hold of his letters and poems, as well as having floated the idea of producing a book, he now took concrete steps to turn their affair into literature, to master her in words as he could not do in reality.[7] On 31 March he sent Lou the first letter of a future book to be entitled *Ombre de mon amour* (*Shadow of My Love*), at the same time musing on the idea of producing a play 'with the impressions I've had since I was here. It's perhaps the best solution to earning a lot of money.' The sequence died out after a second letter on 1 April, but the idea of using his wartime experience was firmly planted.

And so, having resigned from his group of trainee officers and having requested a transfer to the front line, on Easter weekend of 1915 Apollinaire began his long trip to Champagne.

Could the affair have survived? Apollinaire later assured André Rouveyre that there had never been any question of his being in love with the 'houri', although he was not above asking the artist for news of her.[8] On the other hand, the poet's letters do contain passages of great tenderness as well as much evidence of the real practical support he offered Lou, from gifts of money to the use of his flat in Paris. They also demonstrate an at times surprising solicitude for her concerns. Nowhere is this more apparent than in the attempts Apollinaire made to help Lou obtain a *laissez-passer* for her visit to Toutou in February 1915 and in the patience he demonstrated when reassuring Lou that Toutou's appointment as a runner (*agent de liaison*) did not involve significant danger or being transferred to the infantry.[9]

And Lou clearly made an effort to respond, even if Apollinaire would later reproach her for 'all the lies of Nice and Nîmes'.[10] At least in the early days of their affair she was a regular correspondent – the poet received three missives from her on 18 January 1915 – whose letters he variously described as 'lovely', 'astonishingly nice' or in one instance 'extraordinarily suggestive' and whose gifts of fruit he much appreciated. Nor should we underestimate the difficulties that lack of money, a capricious postal system and the uncertainty surrounding leave and travel arrangements would have caused.[11]

However, Lou was also a modern woman whose hard-won independence and sexual freedom she was not about to relinquish. In the second letter of *Ombre de mon amour* Apollinaire wrote that 'I love above all that freedom, that rebellion', but the second part of the sentence suggests a more traditional cast of mind and hints at the difficulties that Lou's independence would cause: 'but I love them in opposition to that very freedom and in opposition to that very rebellion'.

In fact, from fairly early on in their correspondence, the poet's letters began to express his desire to control her, not just sexually (he warns her against masturbation and insists on being told each time she indulges) but in all aspects of her life. 'I don't want to act like a jealous idiot,' he wrote on 29 December. 'There are plenty of things I'll allow you and that I'll allow myself. But I insist that it comes from me.' He scolds her for her lifestyle, he corrects her grammar, meanwhile insisting with increasing frequency on the need for her to subjugate her will to his. 'You are stupidly independent. I must make you bend whether you want to or not.'

Apollinaire's attempts to persuade Lou to join him in Nîmes perfectly illustrate their battle of wills. As early as 26 December the poet had begun to mention rooms in the city in his letters. On 8 January 1915 he said he was going to look for a little flat for her and within two days had been to see a room and sent her full details of the costs. But she clearly pushed back, because on 14

January he wrote that 'you really take me for an idiot, incapable of finding you a place because you're choosy'. However, Apollinaire was not deterred for long. On 20 January he informed her that Madame Nicolini, the wife of his friend in the trainee-officer group, was also going to look for rooms on her behalf.

Then, just as Lou was making her way to the Argonne front, on 7 February Apollinaire dispatched a letter that included a detailed description, including annotated drawings, of an apartment in the Nicolinis' house which he thought would be perfect for her. He had already worked out how meals would be organized, had bought a throw to put over the divan and promised to buy other knick-knacks. It all came to nothing. By late February he had realized that Lou had no intention of taking the accommodation, and he had cancelled the room, paying out sixty francs he could ill afford to recompense the landlord for lost rent.

Meanwhile there was Toutou, whose presence lies behind all the letters of this period. A young, attractive and independent woman like Lou could expect to attract many admirers, and she clearly enjoyed collecting these 'rare flowers' about whose attentions Apollinaire warned her on several occasions. But Toutou was different, a lover to whom Lou would remain constant, emotionally if not sexually, during the time she knew Apollinaire.

Toutou had been on the scene before Apollinaire met Lou, and the poet was careful to establish good relations with him, initially through Lou herself and later through a direct, if limited, exchanges of letters. 'Give me Toutou's news as well,' he wrote to Lou on 23 December, 'since through his love for you and yours for him he's henceforth a part of me.' Apollinaire makes much of the fact that Toutou was already an experienced and more senior artilleryman, expressing his pleasure in Toutou's good opinion of him and vowing to follow any advice he offers.

Quite what Apollinaire imagined (or had persuaded himself)

was the real extent of the friendship between Lou and Toutou is less clear from the letters. There is a surprising comment in Apollinaire's letter of 30 March 1915, for instance, to the effect that 'this delightful shepherd of high-explosive shells [i.e. Toutou] has slept but little with the goddess [Lou].' None the less the extraordinary efforts that Lou made (helped by Apollinaire) in order to visit Toutou at the front and the sheer panic that his designation as a runner engendered in her must have given Apollinaire a clear indication of her feelings.

Likewise, the complex arrangements the poet had to follow in order to correspond with Lou while she was visiting the Argonne front – which included sending letters via Mémée's villa at Saint-Jean-Cap-Ferrat with '*Do not forward*' written on the envelope – proved to be strategies that Apollinaire quickly realized were aimed at obfuscating the part he played in Lou's life. 'I suppose that this comes from the fact that Toutou doesn't know that I write to you every day, and you do the same, and you're afraid of upsetting him.' By mid-March he retained few illusions about his position in her affections. 'I'm delighted he's everything to you, but it's a bit annoying to be nothing at all.'

A final theme of the period between December 1914 and April 1915 was the growing conflict between Apollinaire's sense of honour, as a man from a soldierly lineage, and his feelings for Lou, which had prompted him to promise that he would try to stay in Nîmes. 'I will do nothing to make me leave, I've made you that promise,' he wrote on 27 December. But conquering Lou in love would not be enough.

Because of his age Apollinaire formed part of a reserve, making barrack life something of a backwater. 'Don't forget', he told Lou in late December, 'that there are very few men on active service here. Most of the 3,000 men in our barracks are old and fit for little but guarding the roads and railways.' By early 1915 he was clearly beginning to weigh up whether to apply for a transfer to the front. 'I'll leave you to be the judge and will obey you, but think about my honour,' he told her on 6 January, and this theme was taken up again later in the month.

As their relationship foundered during February 1915 the balance began to tip in favour of departure. 'All things considered I've promised you to do nothing to leave, but it goes without saying that I mustn't do anything to stay.' A crisis point was reached in mid-March when his group of trainee officers was asked for volunteers to serve in Turkey, but Apollinaire turned down the opportunity. 'They asked for two, and it's two others who are going, not me, because, coward that I am, I hadn't any news from you, and I was hoping for some. There's where passion can lead you, my dear friend. *I will never forgive myself for this and will do everything I can to make amends and leave.*'[12] His eventual departure for the front was therefore in many ways a relief. 'I was getting frustrated here. I'm not made to spend much time in a depot. I'd rather go to war and, if I have to die, to die like my ancestors, who were all warriors.'

And so an affair that Apollinaire described at one point as exalted by a 'great poetic and carnal lyricism' wound down. The couple would continue to correspond until January 1916, and there are more than a hundred further letters and poems after March 1915. But the burning fire had been extinguished. André Rouveyre tells of a final brief encounter that proved difficult for both the former lovers, during which a mixture of reproaches and awkward chat left them feeling they would never see each other again – which was indeed the case.[13] But there is no evidence apart from Rouveyre's anecdote that this meeting actually took place.

There is something of a recurring pattern in Apollinaire's life and work. The promise of a '*grand amour*' is followed by expressions of passion with demands for complete surrender and undertones of violence. 'I need your life, your blood, every breath in your body, every one of your desires and the compete agreement of your will, your body, your mind,' he wrote to Lou on 18 January 1915. A sense of disillusionment sets in when that passion is not reciprocated as fully as the poet would wish and the loved one withdraws under the onslaught, all of which is then turned fruitfully into literature with the poet cast as an eternally ill-loved one (*mal-aimé*). This time he would not be returning to his literary pursuits, however, but entering a war zone.

4
CHAMPAGNE
APRIL–JUNE 1915

The poet set off for the front early in the morning of Easter Sunday 4 April 1915 on a journey that was to take almost three days. Such was the volume and complexity of military traffic that rail transport remained painfully slow. Soldiers joked that they could happily accompany their carriages on foot; as Apollinaire wrote in his poem 'Train militaire' ('Troop Train') sent to Lou on 5 April, 'We march, we march with stationary tread.'

A series of postcards and letters allow us to recreate the route: Avignon, Le Teil, Lyon and Dijon on 4 April; Châtillon-sur-Seine (where the train left the Paris–Lyon–Marseille line to join the eastern network), Chaumont and Châlons-sur-Marne on the 5th; and, finally, Mourmelon-Le-Petit in the Champagne region, where the troops disembarked on the 6th. Despite being 'loaded like a mule' and suffering from both lack of sleep and much uncertainty over his ultimate destination (on departure the troops thought they were heading for the Argonne Forest) Apollinaire seems to have enjoyed the journey, describing it as 'almost a pleasure trip'.

He was relieved to now be proving himself neither 'a shirker nor a coward' and proud that, by following his ancestors' military traditions, he was serving both France and his native Poland, 'the country that has suffered most in this war'. It also helped that the poet was accompanied by a close friend and acolyte from the Nîmes barracks who had done his utmost to join him at the front,

René Berthier, a 'poet-corporal', slightly senior to Apollinaire in rank but only twenty-two years old and clearly in awe of the older man whom he regarded as his mentor in poetry.[1] 'Berthier is a young man of great talent,' Apollinaire wrote later, 'a poet and a scientist.' The two friends travelled in first class with four privates and 'laughed and sang like madmen', one way, perhaps, to avoid thinking about what awaited them at the front. Apollinaire's immediate impressions of the journey, mixed with images from the life he was leaving behind, were captured in a free-verse poem he sent to Lou *en route*:

> There are fantastic little bridges
> There's my heart beating for you
> There's an unhappy woman by the road
> There's a lovely little cottage in a garden
> There are six soldiers enjoying themselves like madmen
> There are my eyes searching for your image
>
> There's a charming little wood on the hill
> And an old territorial pisses as we pass
> There's a poet who's dreaming of li'l Lou
> There's an adorable li'l Lou in great big Paris
> There's a battery in a forest
> There's a shepherd who tends his sheep
> There's my life that belongs to you
> There's my fountain pen that flows on and on
> There's an ever so delicate screen of poplars
> There's all my past life that is well and truly past
> There are narrow streets at Menton where we loved each other
> There's a little girl from Sospel who whips her friends
> There's my driver's whip in my feed bag
> There are Belgian carriages on the tracks

There's my love
There's the whole of life
I adore you

The significance – and dangers – of this new period in his life in no way escaped the poet, however. On several occasions he mentions that he will be joining a battery that has been thoroughly 'beaten up'. In a letter sent to his friends Jane and Robert Mortier shortly before his departure he asked them not to leave France so that he would have 'a friendly home to go to' if he came back wounded.[2] Meanwhile a long letter to Lou on 9 April gave detailed advice on the arrangements for his personal effects and his royalties should he be killed.

And there were distinct echoes of his previous leave-taking of Lou in December 1914. Once again Apollinaire seemed deeply saddened by the separation (as was she from what one can glean from his letters). He confessed that anything he had said about two-timing her was false – 'I am as faithful as a guard dog, as I wrote in *Alcools*' – and expressed the hope that she had loved him a little. He looked forward to receiving her 'colours' and wearing them at the front as well as to a future meeting with Toutou, whom he envied. As for his relationship with Lou, he envisaged 'an amazing friendship combined with your agreement with sudden and intermittent carnal pleasures'.

Meanwhile, the reality of war began to intrude. Outside Dijon the train was overflown by a Zeppelin, and all lights had to be extinguished. Wounded troops were seen at stopping points. The countryside was increasingly devoid of civilians – 'profoundly deserted. Nothing but soldiers' – while the landscape lacked the greenery of the south. The villages no longer existed, and war was the only topic of conversation. 'This Champagne is an extremely sad part of the country,' he concluded.[3]

*

The Champagne region, broadly centred on the great cathedral city of Reims, remained critically important to the French High Command throughout the Great War. The area had long been associated with military activity and had been fought over in the early weeks of the conflict, the Germans capturing the city on 5 September 1914.[4] After their subsequent defeat on the Marne the Germans had retreated to the high ground above the river Aisne, establishing a formidable front line that ran just north of Reims eastwards through Souain and on towards the Argonne Forest and Verdun.

To the west of Reims the German-held territory bulged down towards Compiègne and Paris, inviting attacks on its flanks both from Artois and Champagne. In an effort to relieve pressure on their Russian allies the French 4th Army duly launched a poorly prepared attack in the Champagne area on 20 December 1914, which accomplished little more than the capture of some first-line German trenches before it was halted on 13 January 1915.[5] A larger offensive, once more involving the 4th Army, began on 16 February and continued until 20 March. Although the French commander, General de Langle, had 155,000 infantry, 8,000 cavalry and almost 900 guns at his disposal and focused them on a very narrow frontage, the assault again achieved little against the well-established German defence, capturing around three square kilometres of territory at a cost of 43,000 casualties.[6] Apollinaire was not therefore exaggerating when he wrote to Lou that he was going to an area where 'great battles have taken place'.

Apollinaire was by now an artillery driver first class (*1er canonnier-conducteur*) in the 45th battery of his regiment with the rank of lance-corporal, the result of a promotion shortly before his departure for the front.[7] The artillery was organized broadly into different functions. On the front line with the infantry, often less than a hundred metres from the German trenches, were artillery observers who relayed requests for fire support and details of targets back to the firing battery (*batterie de tir*), typically sited around a thousand metres behind the front. Further back, but still within range of enemy artillery and, in some parts of the front, even rifle and machine-gun fire, was the rear unit (*échelon*), where guns not actively in use, as well as other supporting troops, horses and additional equipment (such as a mobile forge) were located.[8] The regimental command and support functions were positioned yet further back from the front line.

Although these different sections were in theory linked by telephone, the wires were constantly cut by shellfire or horses' hooves, so human runners (*agents de liaison*) were employed to carry messages. On arrival at his battery Apollinaire was posted to the rear unit where he would remain stationed until late June. But within days, on 10 April, he became a runner, with responsibility for taking forward messages a couple of times a day, typically to the artillery group commander in the early morning and to an artillery observer in the front-line trenches in the evening.

The position was not without its risks, as his comrades pointed out (one of the previous incumbents had recently been killed), but Apollinaire was delighted to be nominated to this 'junior but dangerous and responsible position'.[9] It gave him, first of all, a sense of worth, of proving useful after only four months in the army. It also held out the possibility of further advancement, although he noted in a letter to Lou on the day of his appointment that 'there are very few promotions in the artillery'. Above all, the poet now had greater freedom to explore the different landscapes of the front within the constraints of his duties, to make chance encounters, to reflect and perhaps even to daydream as he travelled to and fro between the different units on his horse (appropriately named Loulou) and on foot.[10] The following extract from a long free-verse poem called 'Agent de liaison' ('Runner') sent to Lou on

13 April gives a sense of the jumble of images and thoughts going through the poet's mind as he carried out his new role:

> After the bridges the path Careful of the broken
> > Branch
> Ah my heart! Break like a betrayal
> > And here's the broken Branch
> A square of white paper on a bush to the right
> > Where's the square of white paper
> And here I am in front of a hut
> > That is fronted by a flowering profusion
> > Of tulips and narcissi
> Keep right gunner and follow the path
> > At last I'm no longer lost
> > No longer lost
> > > No longer lost
> You can do my Lou whatever you want
> You'll never make my life difficult again my Lou
> A bayonet that could be Hun French or English serves as a poker

The rear unit of the 45th battery, to which Apollinaire had been posted, was stationed in a forest at Beaumont-sur-Vesle, south-east of Reims, in an area of marshy ground. Although some of the poet's early letters play up the literary and frontier aspects of this new life ('I'm thinking of Robinson Crusoe and trappers'), and the artillerymen were certainly more comfortable than their compatriots in the front-line trenches, it was a tough and physically demanding existence.[11] Apollinaire and his comrades had to build their own huts (*cagnats*) from straw and reeds and somehow furnish them: 'You have to be everything: navvy, mason, locksmith, carpenter, everything,' he wrote to Lou on 8 April. Dampness remained a constant problem, not just because of the marshy ground but because a downpour could soak everything, including hut, bedding and kit. At times it was bitterly cold, even as summer approached. 'Here it's got cold again,' he told Lou on 15 May. 'What's more it's raining. I'm frozen, sick to death with waiting about. My hands are like ice.' There was also a great deal of work to do, particularly at night when it was safer to move troops around or to bring up stores. 'Yesterday evening I took off my shoes for the first time since leaving Nîmes,' he wrote on 10 April.

One of the compensating pleasures, particularly for city-dwellers such as Apollinaire, was to discover the wealth of animal life that continued to survive in the war zone despite the constant shelling and bombing.[12] In a letter to his friend Léoncine Havet and her daughters, dated 3 May, the poets lists hares, pheasants, owls, cuckoos, nightingales, herons and grass-snakes.[13] At night glow-worms spangled the roads and fields, and strange insects landed on his notepaper as he wrote. Frogs and toads abounded – as, sadly, did rats, flies and mosquitoes. By late June the poet and his comrades were raising a young bird of prey in imitation of their medieval forebears.

The timing of Apollinaire's arrival at the front also allowed him to witness the profusion of flowers and plant life as spring moved into summer. 'The forest is in its new bloom,' he wrote to his friend André Level on 13 May, 'and everywhere the lilacs are in flower.'[14] An earlier letter to the art-dealer Paul Guillaume listed hazel, cherry, pine and birch among the many variety of trees in the forest, while on 19 May he saw what he believed to be a beautiful flowering hawthorn. 'You would have said a work of art, an artificial plant or one obtained by a particular sort of art, such as the Japanese possess.' The soldiers were able to supplement their rations with morel mushrooms, beetroots and other vegetables grown in small vegetable gardens.

Of course, the main force shaping the landscape was the war itself. In a number of letters Apollinaire describes the war zone as '*fantastique*', a word we should take in the sense of unreal, almost supernatural. Like many soldiers he found the light show at night, with guns firing and star shells bursting, to be extraordinarily compelling. It is 'fairy-like', he told Paul Guillaume in mid-May. But the blasted trees towards the front line (which he likens to pens in a schoolboy's pen-holder), the wicker-and-reed bridges fording the streams and the maze of communications trenches leading up to the front, in which even the most experienced runner could get lost, were equally fantastic.[15] The forward trenches, with their crenellations that resembled ramparts from the Middle Ages, frankly astonished him. 'My God, my God, those battlements are enough to give you nightmares,' he wrote to Lou on 12 April.

War churned up the ground, exposing its geology to view. British images of the conflict are dominated by the mud of Flanders. Mud there certainly was on the Champagne front, but the terrain was predominantly chalky, and Apollinaire makes many references in both his letters and poems to the whiteness of the land, which covered soldiers and their equipment in a powdery dust, particularly in the torrid summer months.[16] A letter to Lou on 21 April described the 'nudity of the trenches [which] has something of the Chinese, of a great Asiatic desert; it's clean and very silently desolate'. Later in the summer he would tell her that the whiteness of the Champagne landscape was so blinding that at times he had resorted to wearing the goggles from his gas mask to avoid the glare.

In the background was the constant roar of artillery and whip-crack of bullets. 'Shelling all day and all night,' Apollinaire wrote to his boyhood friend Toussaint Luca on 20 April. 'Everything thunders, thunders and thunders again,' he told Lou in early May.

He even joked that the presiding deity of the battlefield was 'Obus-Roi' ('Shell-King'), a pun on the title of Alfred Jarry's play *Ubu Roi*. The first stanza of a poem sent to Lou in mid-April captures something of the poet's impressions:

> The sky is spangled with shells from the Hun
> The marvellous forest where I live gives a ball
> The machine gun plays a tune in semiquavers
> But do you have the word – Yes yes the fatal word –
> To the battlements to the battlements leave your pickaxes behind[17]

Yet noise was combined with an extraordinary emptiness on the battlefield itself, as troops on both sides hunkered down in their trenches and bunkers – 'combat where you never see the enemy', as Apollinaire told Paul Guillaume on 16 May. It is no surprise then that the poet sometimes asked himself if everything was real, 'if Gui is Gui, if the earth is the earth and if he hasn't suddenly been transported to another planet'.

What can be gleaned about a soldier's life in the war zone from Apollinaire's letters during his first three months at the front? We need to be cautious, as correspondence was censored, something Apollinaire had anticipated by sending Lou a small set of codes in a letter in early April ('"The weather's good" – will mean "There's a battle"', etc.).[18] He warned her again on 7 April, 'Don't write anything about the war because the letters would be stopped.' By early June the soldiers were being ordered to give fewer and fewer details in their correspondence.

Nevertheless the letters are very revealing.[19] After an initial period of excitement the poet realized that there would now be no let up in his duties. Overwhelming tiredness becomes a recurring theme, partly brought on by Apollinaire's inability to sleep well while surrounded by chirping birds, croaking frogs and scurrying rats, partly as a result of the demands of his life as a soldier. On 16 April, for instance, he spent six hours marching from trench to trench trying to find his forward artillery observer, without success. 'Kilometres, kilometres,' he wrote. Four days later he had to steer his horse through pools of water, liquid lapping up to its knees, and he was almost too tired to write. The need to be constantly on the alert, the unpredictable busyness that left the poet little undisturbed time to himself and meant that letters had to be written in five or six sections, the increasingly harsh discipline imposed at the front ('They're really really tough now,' he told Lou on 24 May) all added to his sense of exhaustion.

Although the Champagne front was now relatively calm after the major offensives launched in the previous December and February danger remained ever present. Even on a quiet day some sixty or seventy enemy shells might arrive and the occasional major bombardment left Apollinaire physically shaken. 'The blasts were repeated so frequently that I felt sick, almost nauseous, and I'm immensely tired,' he wrote on 6 May after one such shelling. The artillerymen at the firing battery seldom ventured out of their bunkers unless it was to fire their guns, such was the effectiveness of German counter-battery fire. But communication lines and even the rear areas were targeted, to the extent that for a period in mid-April Apollinaire was ordered not to travel by horse during the day, forcing him to make all his trips by foot.[20]

By early May Apollinaire was able to write that he was now battle-hardened (*aguerri*) and shells bursting twenty-five metres away no longer bothered him. But there were some close shaves. In a letter to his friend André Level on 25 May the poet described being 'sprinkled' by pieces of shrapnel which fell within a few centimetres of his face, this in the area where the previous runner had been killed. And shellfire was not the only danger. German planes circulated overhead and dropped bombs, one of the few experiences that the poet admitted to finding truly terrifying. The enemy also used gas, against which the French troops had only very basic protection at this point in the war.[21] A letter on the day following a gas attack suggests he had been left 'completely dazed . . . almost stunned'.

Illness, too, was a recurring threat. During periods when no major offensives were under way, all the armies of the Great War lost at least as many troops from their front lines to sickness as to combat. Apollinaire's letters to Lou include discussions about the merits of having a typhoid injection (not yet obligatory in the French Army) and about protection against malaria. On 8 May he wrote, 'There are now a lot of aches and pains in our forest and also eye infections.'[22]

That these dangers were real was constantly brought home by events. The poet's young friend Berthier became exhausted by their living conditions, developed meningitis and in early May 1915 had to be hospitalized for several weeks. In a letter to Toussaint Luca on 20 April Apollinaire acknowledged the death of Luca's brother and another young man, Daniel Escoffier. Meanwhile, an encounter at the front with a handsome young hussar with a rotting foot, for whom the doctors could do nothing – 'he [the doctor] told me that my foot was going to rot and he had nothing to prevent it', the soldier explains – left the poet with a 'horrifying impression'.[23]

In all wars exhaustion and peril combine in a strange way with a sense of monotony and boredom – what Richard Holmes has described as a mixture of work, danger and tedium.[24] Apollinaire's experience was no different, despite the large volume of his correspondence and poems. He speaks of 'the strange banality of a war front' and as early as 8 April suggested to Lou that he might consider transferring to the infantry where 'life doesn't drag'. The lack of movement on the front particularly frustrated him. Anything, even an attack, would be preferable.

So within days of his arrival in Champagne Apollinaire had already been seized by the universal passion among the troops for forging rings and other mementoes from German shells. Female correspondents would henceforth be asked insistently to send their ring measurements. The arrival of the regimental postmaster was eagerly awaited, and any experience that offered something unexpected – attending a religious ceremony presided over by a soldier-priest or seeing a dead horse covered in flies whose buzzing sounded like a 'distant harmonium' – was welcomed and re-created in the poet's letters home.[25]

'Have changed a lot,' Apollinaire tells Lou at one point; 'we poor woodmen have become real savages, and the slightest luxury astonishes us.' It is hardly surprising then that the poet, in common with most front-line soldiers, felt a growing sense of isolation and distance from anyone not directly involved in the conflict. Some misconceptions he found amusing: his mother, he wrote to Lou, 'conceives of war with luxury in mind. A real stroll in the Bois de Boulogne!' But for the shirkers (*embusqués*) in the rear areas, who 'make love as much as they wish, risk nothing and sleep in a nice bed', there was only contempt, a contempt doubtless intensified by the fact that the men in the 45th battery came almost exclusively from the parts of France occupied by the Germans and had no news of their possibly destitute families.[26]

As Jacques Meyer and others have pointed out, the definition of shirker varied greatly depending on your role within the army and did not just include non-combatants. For the infantryman standing in a trench opposite the enemy almost anyone else was a shirker. A particular grievance was that some social groups – farmers, industrial workers – seemed to be doing quite well out of the war in financial terms, while the serving troops were paid very little. In Apollinaire's case his bitterness was directed primarily against the rear-area troops and other able-bodied men enjoying life in his beloved Paris. 'It's quite simply disgusting,' he wrote to Lou.[27] A later poem would describe the capital as a 'bunker where there's too much smiling'.

The propaganda put out by the government-regulated press was also a major source of frustration, as it was for all front-line troops. It was simply not true, he complained to the novelist and editor Eugène Montfort in early June 1915, that German shells did not explode as the newspapers were suggesting. Even the *Mercure de France*, for which Apollinaire had been a regular correspondent, came in for criticism in a letter to Louise Faure-Favier on 24 June for publishing 'too many warlike pedantries written by cowards who don't make us laugh but do make us smile'.

In Apollinaire's case the sense of isolation was increased both by his age and by the difference in background and interests between him and his comrades-in-arms. In a letter to Lou on 20 May he noted that officers tended to be grocers, sergeants, peasant farmers or even 'arch-peasants' (as in comic operas), corporals were peasant farmers or farmhands and the men mechanics, carters or locksmiths. People from liberal careers were paradoxically often simple privates, although there were few of these in his group.[28] That the battery he had joined was largely manned by 'pitiless Picards' from northern France, who spoke a dialect Apollinaire initially had difficulty understanding, was an added barrier.

Apollinaire was therefore downhearted when Berthier was assigned to the firing battery in late April, even though he would see him daily. When the young man was hospitalized with meningitis the older poet was distraught. 'So I'm losing my best, my only, friend here, and an immense void has opened up around me.' The situation was exacerbated by Apollinaire eventually having to share his hut with Sergeant Bodard, 'the most insipid and incorrigible chatterbox on earth'. The poet was reduced to reading silly novels at night until the sergeant went to sleep and left Apollinaire to write letters in peace.

Underpinning the letters from this period, and mirroring the experience of all troops at the front, is an intense sense of sexual frustration. 'We only miss and long for one thing here: WOMEN,' Apollinaire wrote as early as 9 April. As a soldier's song of the period put it:

> Of women
> We have nothing
> Except for Rosalie our bayonet[29]

Later Apollinaire would joke that the most invisible things at the front were Germans and women. Such was the intensity of frustration that men talked openly about having dreamed of sleeping with their sisters or daughters – 'it's a forbidden pleasure in all its horror,' he notes. In a poem included in the same letter to Lou in which these remarks were made Apollinaire spoke of the destruction of 'lascivious flowers', but in his case the flower that had been destroyed was memory, leaving only desire:

> We are ready to die so that you may live
> In happiness
> The shells have burnt away the lascivious flowers
> And that flower
>
> That grew in my heart and is called
> Memory

The ghost of the flower remains
It is desire[30]

Loneliness and sexual frustration perhaps help to explain the extraordinary volume and variety of Apollinaire's correspondence with Lou over this period, despite the adjustment to their relationship they had agreed in late March. Between the poet's departure for the front on 4 April and the end of June he is known to have sent at least seventy-seven cards and letters, twenty of which have poems embedded in the text. Another thirteen self-standing poems and a number of drawings also exist. They provide both a comprehensive diary of his day-to-day experience in the war zone and a chart of the couple's relationship during Apollinaire's first three months as a soldier on active duty.

In many ways their dealings remained very practical. Apollinaire arranged with his landlord and concierge for Lou to stay in his flat while she was in Paris. He advised her on dentists and put her in touch with his mother when Lou needed someone to look after her dogs. He continued to send her money. She, meanwhile, dispatched much-appreciated food parcels to the front and remained a valued source of information about the war rumours circulating in Paris.

At times his letters still presumed an extraordinary level of intimacy to exist between them. He wanted to know details of her menstrual cycle and warned her about venereal disease. On 8 April he sent her an extract from a medical dictionary about 'hypertrophy of the inner lips' (of the vulva) and how this condition could be treated surgically. He directed her to erotic books in his flat and asked her to send him intimate details of her affairs, promising to burn the letters after reading them.

Yet by April he seemed to have accepted both that he would always come second to Toutou in her affections and that she would continue to have casual affairs with her 'rare flowers'. At times he still felt a violent desire for her – 'today great sensuality – desire you a lot, very, very excited', he wrote on 8 May – but he also created almost domestic fantasies in which he and Toutou would look after Lou when the war ended, perhaps even sharing her bed in some sort of sexual 'sandwich'. In the meantime he declared his intention to remain chaste.

As for Lou, if Apollinaire's letters are to be believed, she remained Lou – pleasure-seeking, inconsistent and apparently insensitive to what the poet might be experiencing at the front despite her visits to Toutou in his war zone. At times she wrote that she loved Apollinaire as much as he loved her, that they would have sex again and spend time together when peace finally came.[31] At other times she importuned him for money, scolded him because rumours were circulating in her circle about their time together in Nîmes, accused him of trying to come between her and Toutou and threatened never to speak to him again. Apollinaire wrote in June that he thought Toutou took him for a 'paper soldier' and made fun of him, an impression he clearly suspected Lou had encouraged. He remained critical of what he called her 'frightening and perhaps useless life' and felt obliged to warn her not to steal the books in his flat and to tone down her antics, which he worried might get him evicted after the war.[32] All in all, she continued to leave him deeply puzzled and confused. As he wrote on 19 May, 'I don't understand any more how you treat me. Some days you write to me as if I meant nothing to you, the next day it's a letter of such tender solicitude that it would move a Hun.'

If Apollinaire was increasingly conscious of the gap, both physical and emotional, that was opening between him and Lou – 'such a deep trench', he calls it at one point – his reaction was to possess her in the only way he could, through verse. 'But I don't hate the fact that Love makes me suffer sometimes,' he wrote on 11 April. 'It's an inexhaustible source of poetry.'

As soon as he arrived in Champagne in early April Apollinaire sent Lou a long poem in which he promised to celebrate her beauty. It starts:

> My Lou I shall sleep tonight in the trenches
> Freshly dug and waiting near our guns
> Some twelve kilometers away are the holes
> Where I shall go down in my coat of horizon-blue
> Between the whizzbangs and the casseroles
> To take my place among our soldier-troglodytes
> The train stopped at Mourmelon le Petit
> And I stepped down as happy as I climbed up
> Soon we shall leave for the battery but for now
> I'm among the soldiery and shells are whistling
> In the grey north sky and no one thinks of dying

> *

> And thus we shall live on the frontline
> And I shall liken your arms to the necks of swans
> And sing your breasts belonging to a goddess
> And the lilac shall blossom . . . I shall sing your eyes
> Where a choir of lissom cherubs is dancing
> The lilac shall blossom in the serious spring![33]

Other poems, such as 'Jolie bizarre enfant chérie' ('Pretty Strange Dear Child') where the poet evokes Lou through his five senses, are more explicitly erotic, as the following stanza suggests:

> Pretty strange dear child
> I touch the unique curve of your loins

I follow with my fingers those curves that have made you
Like a Greek statue from before Praxiteles' time
And almost like an Eve in the cathedrals
I also touch the tiny protuberance so sensitive
That is the very essence of your life
It completely annihilates your will through its effects
It is like fire in the forest
It makes you like a giddy flock of sheep
It makes you like an asylum for madwomen
Where the director and chief doctor would become
Mad themselves
It makes you like a placid canal suddenly changed
Into a raging and foaming sea
It makes you like a silky scented soap
That suddenly lathers up in the washer's hands[34]

Later in the poem we find lines that reinforce the idea that Lou is now a projection of the poet's imagination:

So my five senses combine to create you once again
Before me
Even though you are absent and so remote

Lou's presence in the poems is not always positive. At times she appears as a cruel temptress, toying with the poet's emotions:

O cruel Skylark with a vulture's hard heart
You lied yet again to the gullible poet
I listen to the forest moaning in the twilight
The countess went off and then came back one day
Poet adore me but I love another love[35]

Apollinaire's still ambivalent feelings about his former lover may also be discerned in the spectral eroticism of a poem such as 'Les Attentives' ('The Vigilant Ones') which starts:

> He who will die tonight in the trenches
> Is a little soldier whose languid eye
> Observes all day at the cement loopholes
> The Glories which were hung there by night
> He who will die tonight in the trenches
> Is a little soldier my brother and lover
>
> And since he must die I will make myself beautiful
> I want with my naked breasts to set the torches ablaze
> I want with my great eyes to melt the freezing pool
> And my haunches I want to be tombs
> Since he must die I will make myself beautiful
> In incest and in death two such beautiful acts[36]

By early June 1915 Lou was preparing once again to visit Toutou, and Apollinaire was sending out clear warning signals about his relations with her. 'You always write about your problems, never about your pleasures,' he noted. Just as he had become accustomed to the shells sent over by the Germans he now claimed to be indifferent to her gunfire. 'One more physical or emotional shell, I don't give a damn now.' In a letter dated 25 May he had told her that he might try to find 'a less busy heart', since Toutou took up so much space in hers. On 11 June he was more direct. 'It needs a long letter from you, failing which Gui will get quieter and quieter, demoralized by Lou's indifference.'

This time it was no idle threat. Between late June 1915 and the end of their relationship early in the following year Apollinaire would write no more than thirty letters to Lou. In April the poet had set off a correspondence which, although radically different in nature to that with Lou, would prove equally significant, both for him and his poetry. Madeleine Pagès had arrived on the scene.

They met on the train from Nice to Marseilles on 2 January 1915. Apollinaire was returning to his barracks in Nîmes after his brief leave spent with Lou. In a short memoir written to accompany the first publication of the poet's letters to her in 1952 Madeleine recalled that Lou joined Apollinaire briefly in the train compartment at Nice station, while she stepped discreetly into the corridor to allow the lovers to say their goodbyes.[37]

Madeleine, too, had spent the holiday period in the city with her sister-in-law, whose husband, Madeleine's older brother, had been called up into the artillery. She was now travelling back via Marseille to Lamur, near Oran in Algeria, where she lived with her widowed mother and five other brothers and sisters. She was twenty-two and a language assistant in a girls' secondary school in Oran.[38] In a letter written to Lou on that same day Apollinaire described the young woman as 'pretty intelligent what's more, and honourable I think'.

According to Madeleine's memoir she and Apollinaire were alone for the first part of the journey and struck up a conversation that rapidly turned to the subject of poetry. When she told him that she 'loved it as much as life itself and, in any case . . . didn't make a distinction between them', she thought Apollinaire was almost ready to kiss her. Before long the couple were reciting their favourite lines to each other or in tandem. Another traveller joined them, taking the conversation in a different direction (Apollinaire discovered that the man had been a fellow student of his brother Albert), but left alone again later in the journey the poet and the young woman began to trade images – Nice as a 'rearing horse', Villefranche as a 'large open seashell'.[39] Eventually Apollinaire confessed that he, too, was a poet, which thrilled her, although she was embarrassed to admit that she had never heard of him. He took her address – she rather daringly missed off the Mademoiselle in front of her name – and promised to send her a copy of his book *Alcools*. At Marseille station she rushed off in a fluster 'like a badly brought up little girl or, even more horrendous, like a little thing from the provinces with no manners'. A storm during the crossing to Oran mirrored her 'first tempest'.

This initial meeting prefigured many of the elements of the ensuing correspondence. Madeleine was overwhelmed to meet a man of such erudition and sophistication with whom she could share her literary passions. And a published poet – how could she not be entranced? But at the same time she was fearful, initially cautious, perhaps even suspicious. After all he was twelve years older, a soldier and had already shown he had a lover.

Apollinaire, meanwhile, was delighted to find an attractive young woman whom he could amuse and talk to about literature, whose personality and body (unlike Lou's) he had scope to create largely through his words and imagination since they had spent so little time together and who would join him in developing an epistolary relationship that has been described as one founded on the myth of a love that was both instantaneous and ideal;[40] but who, the poet recognized almost instinctively, must not be frightened away as their correspondence became increasingly intimate. Apollinaire therefore had to put all the powers of his pen to the service of love, showing himself at times demanding, passionate and direct, at others courteous, relaxed and open-minded.[41]

The correspondence was slow to start. Only on 16 April 1915 did Apollinaire dispatch a card apologizing for the delay in sending the promised copy of *Alcools*. Madeleine replied with a parcel of provisions that reached the front on 4 May, and the letters became more frequent from then on. There are five letters from Apollinaire in May, nine in June despite a gap when the battery was changing sectors.

The tone in these initial letters is immediately distinct from that adopted with Lou. For a start, Apollinaire addresses Madeleine as *Mademoiselle* and uses the polite *vous* form. While he provides descriptions of the landscape and life at the front, just as in his correspondence with Lou, he makes much greater use of classical and literary references to Homer and Oedipus, Cervantes and Gogol, at one point discussing the difficulties of reading master-pieces such as *Paradise Lost*. In only his third letter, on 20 May, he sketched out his ideas on the use of regular verse, arguing that audaciousness should in no way mean ignorance of past literature. On the other hand, style, he argued, meant only discipline and personality; otherwise you were merely copying previous work of art: 'Can(n)ons', he puns, 'are only useful in artillery.' Clearly, with Madeleine he had a different audience.

And yet he was almost more demanding emotionally than with Lou, perhaps reflecting the anxieties caused by life at the front. By his second letter he was calling Madeleine 'little fairy' and requesting both her ring measurements and a photograph, which he said he would carry on the same side as his sabre and revolver (and therefore next to his heart). Later he would send her a lock of his hair as a way of suggesting he would like a lock of hers. On 20 May the poet complained that he had found her latest letter 'less good and less gentle than the previous one', but he quickly realized he had gone too far and asked her forgiveness a few days later. A free-verse poem sent on 28 May and entitled 'Madeleine' combines an evocation of their Mediterranean train ride and camp life with a pun on the word 'love' (to coil like a snake in French):[42]

It is a thing so tenuous so distant
That even just thinking about it can make it too solid
A form bounded by the blue sea
By the sound of the wheels of the train
By the smell of eucalyptus of mimosa
And maritime pine

But the contact and the savour

And this alert little traveller with a quick nod on the platform
    of the Marseilles train station
        Went off
        Not knowing
That her memory would hover
Over a little wood in Champagne where a soldier
Beside the fire of a bivouac tries to conjure up that apparition
Through the birch bark's smoke
Which smells of Minean incense
While the bluish scrolls
From a cigar write the sweetest of names
But the snakes slipping their knots
Also write the touching name
Whose every letter flows in a beautiful round English hand

And the soldier doesn't dare put an end
To the bilingual wordplay that this sylvan
And vernal calligraphy cannot not conjure up

The young woman was clearly unsure exactly how to respond to this epistolary assault. She sent him a photograph and began to sign her letters with her first name but then reverted to M. Pagès, the poet meanwhile addressing her as *mademoiselle* once again in his letter of 3 June. On the following day Apollinaire apologized for upsetting her (she had been in tears) and begged her to take back her threats to cut off contact. They agreed that they would keep their letters secret from family and friends.

By mid-to-late June some sort of crisis was clearly approaching. She had written to him to say that she was less free than he perhaps imagined and she would not give him a promise she could not keep. 'What promise have I asked for?' the poet responded rather disingenuously. On 22 June he advised her not to be coy and declared himself very anxious over her hesitations. He set out his very traditional views on marital roles (perhaps sensing she required this reassurance) and pressed her to declare her feelings. On the following day he commented on two new photographs she had sent him, imagining the corsetless body beneath the clothes.

Before the situation could be resolved, however, Apollinaire's battery underwent a major change in disposition to another more terrifying section of the front. He also published his first major collection of poems from the war.

Apollinaire's first three months at the front proved remarkably fruitful not just in correspondence but in verse, resulting in some sixty-five poems fairly evenly spread across April, May and June. In fact from the beginning of his time in Champagne the poet was conscious of a renewal in his inspiration.[43] A recurring theme in his correspondence around this time is that life in the war zone, for all its horrors and hardship, was worth being lived, as he wrote to the poet and novelist Fernand Fleuret on 19 April. The poem 'En allant chercher des obus' ('On Going to Look for Shells'), sent to Lou on 13 May, begins with the poet addressing himself thus:

You who go before the long convoy marching in step
In the clear night
Your testicles full your brain replete with new images . . .

A poem from later in June, 'Oriande', contains the lines:

The old words died last spring
New and powerful harmonies gush from my heart

If inspiration was renewed and poetry was once again central to Apollinaire's preoccupations, how could he best guard against the loss of his work in the potentially deadly turmoil of the front? One way was to send copies of poems to several recipients, something for which Apollinaire has sometimes been criticized but which seems, on reflection, an entirely practical response to his dilemma. The other option, of course, was to publish.

On 1 June 1915 Apollinaire announced to Lou that he was preparing a small book that would be sold on subscription, with her as the beneficiary of any income it raised. Selling twenty copies at twenty francs each would meet her dental bills, he suggested. At this stage a print run of 112 copies was envisaged. Three days later the run had been reduced to sixty, and the book had a name, *La case d'armon*, eventually to become *Case d'armons (Limber Store)*. The title is significant, the *case d'armons* being the small section in an artillery limber where gunners could stow their personal effects. An area of privacy and intimacy therefore on a fearsome machine devoted to war as well as a distinguishing feature of the artillery-man (the infantry carried everything on their backs).

In the end, perhaps because the regiment was about to change position, only twenty-five copies of the volume could be produced, with a publication date of 17 June. A plan to share the proceeds between wounded troops and the men in Apollinaire's battery with families in the occupied zone (the ambition communicated to everyone apart from Lou) also had to be abandoned when the poet discovered that soldiers on active service were banned from undertaking any form of commercial activity. The copies were mainly distributed to friends.

That the volume of twenty-one poems was produced at all remains something of a miracle, given the shortages at the front of basics such as paper and ink (the latter was often replaced by soot and water). Using material normally destined for the 45th battery's newspaper, the *Tranchman'Echo*, and working from Apollinaire's original manuscripts (now lost), the poet's two friends, the faithful Berthier and the 'incorrigible chatterbox' Lucien Bodard, copied out the poems by hand on to squared letter paper to form a dummy publication, adding little drawings and illustrations of their own devising.[44] The twenty-five copies were then run off using a gelatine process – 'at the firing battery . . . facing the enemy', according to a covering page. There are slight variations in the page order of the different copies, and Apollinaire himself inked in letters that had come out too pale. In some cases he also made discreet changes to the text, for instance, taking out references to Madeleine in the version sent to Lou. All of which means that each of the copies is unique, and *Case d'armons*, as the poet in fact envisaged, has become one of the rarest of rare books.

Paradoxically the difficult conditions in which *Case d'armons* was produced proved favourable to finding new ways of expressing Apollinaire's impressions, sensations and experiences at the front. As duplication rather than printing was involved the poet was able to send his lines in different directions, to form shapes with words and letters, to add drawings and elements of collage. The poem 'Carte postale' ('Postcard'), for instance, involved the use of an actual military postcard, while 'SP' incorporated in an ironic way extracts from official instructions on how to combat a gas attack.[45]

AIM

For Madame René Berthier

Cherry-color horses boundary of Zeeland

Machine guns of gold are croaking legends

I love you liberty keeping watch in the catacombs

Harp with silver strings oh rain oh my music

The invisible enemy a silver wound in the sunlight

And the secret future a flare illuminates

Listen to the Word swim subtle fish

The cities one by one become keys

My blue mask as God puts on his sky

War peaceful ascesis metaphysical solitude

Child with severed hands among roses oriflamme

The converging lines of 'Visée' ('Aim') could be shells homing in on a target, the image of an artillery sighting instrument, a spray of machine-gun fire or even a representation of a flag.[46]

All the poems Apollinaire wrote in the war zone manifest an astonishing diversity of form. The freedom of invention and broad range of themes addressed in *Case d'armons* can therefore be seen as emblematic of the radical innovations the poet was introducing into his work during this period. The poet combines elements of the war with his own personal mythology, using techniques that give the reader ever greater freedom to move within the text, prompt many different interpretations and even increasingly separate the text in a poem from any accompanying *calligrammes*. He borrows military terms and place names, exploits different styles including that of army communications and uses typography and layout to suggest graffiti, military hardware or topographical features.

The poem 'Venu de Dieuze' ('On Arrival from Dieuze'), for example, incorporates references to Apollinaire's daily life at the front – the exchanging of passwords, the neighing of horses in the marshy landscape, the Picard patois spoken by his comrades in the battery. There are musical symbols and references to popular song, the Marseillaise and the notes of the reveille. The last two lines may contain a subtle criticism of the French commander Joffre's cautious approach to the war, one of the Roman generals named Fabius being a notorious temporizer. At the same time elements of the divine intrude, perhaps suggesting the battlefield is a sacred space. Dieuze is the name of a town in eastern France but is also a feminized form of the word *Dieu* (God), while *Claire-Ville-Neuve-En-Cristal-Eternel* may be a reference to the celestial Jerusalem of the Apocalypse.[47] The importance of '*Le Mot*' (translated as password) may reflect not just the life-or-death power of passwords and military orders but also Apollinaire's views on the vital creative

Halt

finger side

Who goes there

France

Advance to the rally

Halt

The Password

Shining- New- City- in- Eternal- Crystal

rope-dancer shell
in the rings
of springtime
you kill
the trees that are
your G.V.C. The moor
then clucks and dips
at your approach

Cantato { Oh God! my little girl
That man of mine
What a fly in the ointment
Absolutely

forte sull'andante

Swamp butterflies   sky-blue mushrooms
Whinnies   everywhere.
Sacred love   patriotic love
          The general
He was Antisthenes and Fabius as well

role of poetry. All of this is presented using very untraditional layout and typography.[48]

This poem and others in the collection are not therefore panegyrics to war, as some of Apollinaire's critics were later to claim but, rather, an exaltation of the creative powers of the poet faced with a conflict that is unprecedented in its scope, destructiveness and absurdity.[49] As the poet strives to express the full range of his and his comrades' experience he must invent new poetic forms in which to do so, since the nature of the war has rendered obsolete traditional representations such as the epic.[50]

5
CHAMPAGNE
JULY–NOVEMBER 1915

At midnight on 27 June 1915 Apollinaire's battery left the Beaumont-sur-Vesle area and began a three-day journey to the fiercely contested sector around Les Hurlus, some thirty kilometres further east. He would remain on this part of the front until December.

The going was hard, but Apollinaire seems to have appreciated the adventure almost as much as his original train ride from the south. 'We slept under the stars; for the moment we're sleeping under canvas, on the ground. I've really enjoyed it all,' he wrote to Lou on 1 July, while he later described the regimental move in almost lyrical terms to the artist Pierre Roy. 'I did three sectors with the guns limbered up these night-time trips were magnificent, under the brilliantly doleful glances of the Hun's searchlights, while white, red and blue star shells were bursting and the big shells were caterwauling.'[1]

The landscape that the battery now entered was less than magnificent, however. Something of a wasteland before 1914, the Hurlus sector was now 'a sinister place, where alongside all the horrors of war, the horror of the location, the frightening abundance of cemeteries sits the lack of trees, of water, even of real earth', Apollinaire told Madeleine on 1 July. 'Beelzebub is here with his legions,' he wrote on the following day, 'his infinite myriads of green, blue, brown flies.'[2]

While the regiment's previous position near Beaumont had allowed at least some contact with local villages such as Verzy and

Verzenay, which were slowly being repopulated despite the daily German shelling, the 'Gehenna' in which Apollinaire and his comrades now found themselves offered only 'solitude in all its horror'. Here was nothing but 'super-metallic, all-thundering war itself', in Apollinaire's memorable phrase;[3] here French and German troops lived in 'putrid holes', their lines so near one another that there was a constant exchange of grenades and you hardly had to show your head above the parapet to be killed. As Apollinaire told Lou on 23 July, a battalion could quickly melt away without being involved in any attacks, merely as a result of the 'perpetual butchery'.

Isolation meant a massive increase in work for the troops, despite the *échelon* being only some 1,200 metres from the firing battery. Even watering the horses involved a fourteen-kilometre round trip to the rear, which had to be done twice daily. And in the process of moving camp the men had had to leave behind much of their carefully accumulated *matériel* and were once again faced with constructing their own shelters and furniture in an area where the means to do so were difficult to come by.[4] While assuring Lou and Madeleine that he was quite cheerful, Apollinaire was at the same time writing to Paul Guillaume that he was in 'a bad, bad, bad way here'. A poem 'Cote 146' ('Hill 146') sent to Madeleine on 2 July reflects this shock of this new sector:

Plains Desolation fly-blown hell Flares green white and red
50-shell salvos in the trenches like when four of you beat a large carpet
    to rid it of its dust
Craters like Gothic cathedrals
Humming of aggressive flies
Letters encased in a cigar box sent from Oran
The water detail returns with its casks
And the wounded men return alone through the huge arid
    communication trench

Branch line of the Decauville railway

Over there they're playing hide and seek

We're playing blind man's buff

Beautiful dreams

Madeleine what is not devoted to love is such a waste of time

Your photos next to my heart

And the metal flies little stars at first

On horseback on horseback on horseback on horseback

O plain craters everywhere where men stagnate

O plain where the communication trenches are scored like fingerprints
    on the monumental Gavrinis stones

Madeleine your name like an indistinct rose rose of the winds or of the
    rose bush

The drivers go off to the watering hole 7 km from here

Perthes Hurlus Beauséjour pale names and you Ville sur Tourbe

Soldiers' cemeteries crosses where the kepi weeps

The shadow is made of putrefied flesh the sparse trees are dead men left
    standing

Hear the shell weep as it passes overhead[5]

The move to the new sector did, however, offer some com-
pensation in the form of promotions. Having arrived at the front
as a first-class artillery driver Apollinaire quickly assumed the role
of runner (*agent de liaison*) and had become a full corporal by mid-
April. 'At the depot I really worked hard, so much so that I've been
able to make myself useful here,' he explained to the novelist
Eugène Montfort.[6] On 18 July he was appointed quartermaster
corporal (*brigadier-fourrier*) for his battery, responsible for matters
such as stores, lodging and correspondence. As he told both Lou
and Madeleine this was a sought-after if time-consuming position
that involved a lot of contact with the battery captain and artillery
group commander but in return absolved the postholder from

fatigues such as the daily watering runs as well as offering a good deal of freedom. By now versed in army politics the poet seems to have left any accounting work to the other quartermaster while taking on most of the other tasks himself, an arrangement that ensured a harmonious relationship.

Further promotion followed in the latter part of August when Apollinaire was appointed sergeant (*maréchal des logis*) with effect from 1 September. Before taking up his new position, however, he spent a week as a flash spotter (*observateur aux lueurs*). Having entered the war behind the Germans in terms of counterbattery capabilities the French Army was, by the autumn of 1915, creating special artillery-intelligence units in each of its major front-line formations to provide information for operations against enemy gun emplacements.[7] As a flash spotter Apollinaire had to take up position in 'an observatory situated on a desolate ridge sprinkled by shellfire . . . So I spend the night in this observatory where I direct the alidade of the sighting triangle on the flashes from the Hun's guns.' Although tiring and painstaking – the enemy coordinates had to be recorded carefully – the work offered the poet a bird's-eye view of what he calls 'the opera' of the front at night, 'a continuous and barbarous music, French and Hun cannon-fire of all calibres, rifle shots, machines guns. The flashes from the firing lit up the sky, the hard jets of light from the searchlights moved across the sky like strangely elongated actors who came closer went back grew larger grew smaller the star shells the lingering signals raining fluttering spherical white orange blue green climbed up, like strange and exquisite dancing girls.'[8] A free-verse poem entitled 'Lueurs' ('Flashes'), sent to Madeleine on 10 September, uses a detailed description of the technical process and the landscape surveyed as a metaphor for poetic activity and creativity:

Your watch is beside the candle that gutters behind a screen made with
the tin-plate from a jam container
In your left hand you hold the chronometer that you'll start at the
appropriate moment
You hold yourself ready with your right hand to point the alidade of the
sighting triangle at the sudden distant flashes
As you point you start the chronometer and you stop it when you hear
the shell-burst
You note the time the number of shots the calibre the deflection the
number of seconds elapsed between the flash and the detonation
You watch without turning away you watch through the embrasure
The flares dance the bombs explode and the flashes appear
While the simple and rough symphony of the war ascends
So in life my love we point our heart and our fervent attention
At unknown and hostile flashes that decorate the horizon populate it
and govern us
And the poet is that spotter of life and invents the countless flashes of
mysteries that must be located
Understood oh Flashes oh my dearest love

'My dear, I'm now a sergeant and I'm very proud of this promotion,' Apollinaire wrote to Madeleine once his new appointment had been confirmed. 'Who could have persuaded you a couple of years ago that I would become an expert in the art of deploying artillery and that I would be in command of firing a gun,' he later asked Eugène Montfort.[9] For his promotion had put the poet in charge of the battery's fourth gun, and he was no longer in the rear unit, where he had left his horse as well as most of his belongings, but forward in the firing battery.

He now lived beside his artillery piece and commanded a crew that included six gunners, a telephonist, a secondee from the engineers, who managed the searchlights, and a supernumerary

NCO in case one of the crew was killed. 'I'm head of the family,' he wrote to his friend André Billy on 10 September.[10] At night he and his gunners slept in a dug-out that was 'completely underground and surmounted by a thick earth bulwark built over logs' and which was directly connected by a trench to the gun, itself under cover.

Food, he would later tell Eugene Montfort, was prepared by one of the gun crew and in the simplest of ways, 'but it's healthy and plentiful; it's the daily stew'.[11] Life was circumscribed in other ways, too: great care had to be taken not to give the gun position away to the German observation balloons and planes that were constantly overhead. A short free-verse poem entitled 'Chef de pièce' ('Gun Commander'), sent to Madeleine on 3 September, described this new life:

> The sarge is at his gun
> He sleeps in his shelter beside the cannon
> He lives with his gunners and shares their grub
> He writes next to them to Madeleine
> He plays with all seven of them like children
> He thinks about the Big Show that is coming
> He admires the marvellous enthusiasm of the squaddies
> Courage has really grown everywhere
> And everyone's sure everyone's certain about the Big Show
> He'll be thinking all the while of Madeleine[12]

It was as a gun commander therefore that Apollinaire participated in one of the great offensives of 1915 (the Big Show in the poem above): the Second Battle of Champagne.

Italy's entry into the war on the side of the Allies in May 1915 had provided a glimmer of light in an otherwise dark year, both diplomatically and militarily, for the Western Powers. Operations in Gallipoli against the Turks had become bogged down; the German and Austro-Hungarian armies were advancing relentlessly against the Russians, with Warsaw falling on 5 August; and German diplomats were making very active efforts in the Balkans that would eventually result in Bulgaria joining their war effort on 6 September. The Western High Command was therefore under intense pressure to act, both to support their Russian comrades and to persuade neutrals that they were not losing the war. A major success in Champagne would meet both objectives as well as opening a path into the occupied territories.

During the summer of 1915 the French Army reorganized and expanded, bringing new men, artillery and ammunition to the front line as well as developing new techniques in aircraft reconnaissance and artillery spotting. For the offensive the Champagne front was divided between two armies – De Langle's 4th Army facing the area to the west of Perthes and Pétain's 2nd Army, to which Apollinaire's regiment was assigned, to the east. The offensive was originally planned for late August, but preparations for large-scale operations always took time, and the start date was postponed first to 8 September and then until the 25th. Unfortunately the delay not only gave the Germans plenty of time to gather intelligence on the French plans but allowed them to develop yet further a formidable three-mile-deep defensive system whose second-line position on the reverse slope of the hills north of the French lines largely protected it from French artillery fire.[13]

A heavy-artillery bombardment began on 22 September in preparation for the offensive, and the infantry moved forward at 9.25 a.m. on the 25th after a night of heavy rain that would continue, with only brief respites, for the following four days.[14] The main French successes came early. By the end of the 26th the

2nd and 4th Armies had advanced between three and four kilometres on a 27-kilometre frontage and had captured some 18,000 prisoners. The territorial gains were not insignificant – la Main de Massiges, la Ferme de Navarin, Tahure, les Deux Mamelles, Souain – and at the very least deprived the Germans of important observation points in the sector. But the German second line remained intact and halted any further forward movement. The offensive was temporarily suspended at the end of September, but on 4 October artillery fire in support of a new attack began, and the infantry moved forward once again at 5.20 a.m. on the 6th. By late the following day, however, it was clear that the troops had come to a halt, and the High Command terminated operations. On one estimate, between 25 September and mid-October the French lost 27,851 men killed, 53,658 captured or missing and 98,305 wounded.[15]

Despite playing a very active part in what he would later describe as 'the greatest artillery battle of all time' Apollinaire still found time to continue his voluminous correspondence during this period.[16] The letters give an insight into both the hopes that the troops invested in the attack and the preparations they were required to make.

A first indication that something was happening came in mid-July when the poet and his comrades transferred from the 4th to the 2nd Army. In mid-August the battery then changed location, although within the same sector, and Apollinaire now found himself in 'a beautiful forest of fir, juniper, warty spurge, fir [*sic*] and moss', as a card to Madeleine announced on 16 August. The new position had an abundance of spiders but mercifully few flies, and the poet's relief was palpable, despite the tricky terrain ('charming life but dangerous terrain when it rains. The ground is as slippery as soap,' he told Lou on 18 August) and the heavy workload. 'Don't have a minute's rest, just the time to grab a bite, manual work, on the battery and hardly anything for me.'

By early September, and with Apollinaire now in place as a gun commander in the firing battery, preparations were becoming increasingly intense. 'We did ranging fire with planes,' he told Madeleine on the 5th; 'it's a lot of fun.' New equipment was arriving – cagoules to replace the rudimentary gas masks previously supplied to the troops and new Adrian steel helmets, which he found 'extremely protective and pleasant to wear although pretty heavy'. He sent his kepi to Madeleine for safekeeping. More ominously, he warned her that all leave was suspended, which would delay any trip to Algeria, and he was likely to be out of touch even with his rear unit at times.[17]

Meanwhile, the Germans were clearly doing their utmost to disrupt the French preparations to the point where replenishment of the firing battery's supplies became impossible on 8 September, and the crew had to live on basic rations. Two days later Apollinaire wrote to André Billy that the Germans were no longer firing medium 77-millimetre artillery shells but 'nothing but big shells that make a devil of a noise and cave in a bunker in five seconds'.[18] They were also using gas to disrupt the French artillery, and Apollinaire and his comrades had frequently to wear their cagoules.

What is striking about the letters from this period is their optimism. Apollinaire had complained earlier in the summer about the French Army's passivity; now there was an opportunity to land a fatal blow on the enemy. 'Here the war continues,' he wrote to Madeleine on 5 September. 'It's going to become more decisive; what marvellous morale at the moment!' Ten days later he remained confident. 'This time I've the greatest confidence, it will be the last great push. I believe this, and it's what people are saying.'

This sense that the decisive battle was at hand carried over into the offensive itself. On the first day of the artillery bombardment, 22 September, Apollinaire wrote to Lou about 'the Big Show which can only end in a great victory'. During the following few days, as well as maintaining 'an almost interrupted fire' the battery was constantly on the alert to move forward to new positions. 'We leave tomorrow for the occupied territories. We saddled up last night. The equipment is ready, and the limbers have been provided with fascines to bridge the trenches,' he told Madeleine on the 24th. Meeting and chatting to German prisoners, whom he found very young, badly dressed and obsequious, reinforced his belief that the French were doing well.

That the call to advance never seemed to come did not initially dampen the poet's optimism. On 28 September he told Lou that victory was assured, that he was ' helmeted, spurred' and waiting to move forward and that he was 'almost drunk with this long battle that's already lasted 7 days'. On the 30th he spoke to Madeleine about 'the extraordinary bombardment that so surprised the Hun'. But by the time he wrote to her on 6 October his mood seemed heavier, even though another attack was imminent. If there was still talk of moving, it would not be far; the regiment had rejoined its old army corps (itself perhaps a sign that the offensive was winding down); nothing was certain.[19] The letter included a poem 'Désir' that interwove his desire for her with the desire (now fading?) for victory and an advance through German lines:

My desire is the region that is before me
Behind the Boche lines
My desire is also behind me
Beyond the zone of the armies

My desire is the butte de Tahure
My desire is the place I fire at
As for my desire that is beyond the zone of the armies
I'm not mentioning it today but I think about it

CHAMPAGNE, JULY–NOVEMBER 1915

Butte de Tahure I imagine you in vain
Barbed wire, machine-guns, Huns too cocksure
Too ensconced underground already buried

Tac tac tac, shots dying away as they disappear

Keeping watch late into the night
The Decauville that splutters
Corrugated iron in the rain
And in the rain my helmet

Hear the vehement earth
See the flashes before hearing the shots
And some shell whistling like a thing gone mad
Or the monotonous short rat-a-tat full of disgust

I see you Main de Massiges
So emaciated on the map

The Goethe Trench on which I've fired
I've even fired on the Nietzsche Trench
All and all I have no respect for greatness

Violent and violet and dusky night and at times resplendent with gold
Night for men alone
Night of 24 September 1915
Tomorrow the attack
Violent night, oh night whose deep terror-ridden cry was growing ever
    more intense
Night for men alone
Night that was screaming like a woman in labour[20]

In the months following the offensive – in fact, until the great struggles of 1918 – Champagne became a secondary front. But this did not mean it was calm. There were almost daily artillery duels, and a series of German counter-attacks during October came close to regaining the ground that the French had won at such cost. However, by 3 November the situation was sufficiently under control for Apollinaire and his men to begin a move forward a short distance north-west into the newly captured territory around Trou Bricot.

Once again the landscape was horrific, 'the most deserted region of the front, since it was a desert even before the war'. There were plagues of rats and mice, and gas was so prevalent that Apollinaire began to find that the smell was no longer unpleasant. Initially the poet and his gun crew seem to have camped out with their rear unit in awful conditions, since in the expectation of a rapid advance following the September offensive all but essential equipment had been abandoned: 'Just imagine the rain and the snow on all the poor soldiers with nothing but their canvas. As for me, I was in an old hut that looked like the sort of crib you make in churches for Christmas.' It was with some relief that on 17 November Apollinaire and his comrades finally took up their firing positions in a captured German dug-out, which the poet told Madeleine was 'the most pleasant that I've found until now'.[21] 'We had no regrets leaving the *échelon* because we were freezing there and slept in water,' he would add later.

On a less happy note, the new position was in the middle of a large German cemetery and next to a small French one. Apollinaire was fascinated by the well-made German tombs and the rose bushes in the NCOs' area, each with a little label naming the type of rose. However, in this 'Shakespearian scenery' horror was never far away, and on 19 November a shell disinterred a German 'whose tibia pokes out from earth-covered funeral rags'.

Meanwhile, a hard northern winter was setting in. Already on 3 November Apollinaire had sent Madeleine a long description of the mud. 'What mud, what mud ... sometimes with the consistency of mastic, sometimes of whipped cream sometimes again of wax polish and extraordinarily slippery. You have to have seen the teams falling down, getting up under the drivers' whips or breaking the reins when the fall is too sudden.' On 14 November the white countryside became even whiter with the first snowfall. 'Everything that wasn't white, and God knows there's enough white in this chalky countryside that's been terribly churned up more than a year of war, became white all of a sudden.' With a failed offensive behind him, living in a charnel house and with the horror of winter to come, for the first time the poet really began to express an unconditional desire for the arrival of peace, 'this peace I'm beginning to wish for with all the breath in my body'. The following extract from a poem sent to Madeleine on 18 November, and called 'Chevaux de frise' after the large barbed-wire obstacles found on the front, captures something of the poet's increasingly urgent desire to be elsewhere with his beloved:

> During the white and nocturnal November
> While the trees the artillery had hacked
> Aged even more as the snow fell
> They weren't even chevaux-de-frise
> Surrounded by waves of barbed wire
> My heart was being reborn like a tree in spring
> A fruit tree on which love's flowers
> > Are coming into bloom
>
> During the white and nocturnal November
> While the shells were horribly singing
> And earth's dead flowers exhaled

> Their mortal odours
> Every day I'd describe my love to Madeleine
> Snow puts pale flowers on the trees
> And tufts of ermine on the chevaux-de-frise
> You see them everywhere
> Abandoned and sinister
> Mute horses
> Not Barb horses but barbed wire
> And suddenly I can bring them to life
> A pretty troop of piebald horses
> Galloping towards you like white waves
> On the Mediterranean
> Bringing you my love[22]

At the end of June 1915 Apollinaire had been pressing Madeleine for an avowal of her feelings towards him. Her response came in early July, and on the 10th he was able to write to her that 'I love you, too, Madeleine, and I loved you from the moment I saw you.' Things moved quickly thereafter. By 12 July the poet was aware that Madeleine had spoken to her mother who did not disapprove of this 'long-distance exchange of views'. A fortnight later the question of his leave began to arise, and by early August she was writing daily, while he had sent her a marriage proposal and was awaiting 'a letter, *the letter*'. On 10 August, after an anxious exchange with his beloved, the poet wrote a formal letter to her mother requesting Madeleine's hand in marriage ('Words fail me,' he told her, surely one of the few times Apollinaire was ever tongue-tied). Fortunately Mme Pagès responded favourably, and by 20 August the poet was addressing her daughter as his 'little fiancée, whom I desire so much spiritually but carnally, too (it has to be said)'.

This betrothal unleashed an exchange of letters that, even today, is startling in its intensity and explicitness. In the virginal

Madeleine, still almost adolescent in her worries about being ugly and stupid and in her lack of knowledge about sex (at one point Apollinaire refers to her clitoris as 'the little hermit whose existence you were unaware of'), the poet would eventually discover the inventive, unbridled, even courageous correspondent that he had long hoped to find in Lou. She would become a correspondent who by mid-November was willing to send the poet a 'dear description of [her] threshold', from which he promised to drink champagne, and to whom he felt able by then to offer the tenth in a series of extraordinarily frank and erotic free-verse 'secret poems':

My love is on her knees her legs parted
Her head is buried in the cushions
My love's black hair spreads around her like a thousand snakes emerging
    from their nests
My love arches her back and lifts up her buttocks as far as she can
So that the master sees between her thighs
The clump of forest on the curved dome that crowns the sap I wish to take
Bees live there and the sweetest honey is fermented
Her buttocks extend their polar whiteness and appear in all their
    splendour
And today my mouth wants to take another sap which opens small and
    dark
In the long deep trench
That separates the two mountains of your buttocks
My tongue lingers there unfolding the secret folds
And you stretch out obligingly delighted by this first homage this unique
    caress never offered to others this unique rare and delicious caress
And then oh my slave sensing that you are truly reassured truly mine
I bring the sapper near to the little sap
He enters gently and only with his head and you raise up your head so
    that your mouth can seek mine

My right hand caresses your breasts and my left makes off to awaken
    your pleasure in the depths of the mysterious forest
While the sapper goes back and forth in the most secret lair and your
    crystal buttocks beat time against my belly
Until the moment when the mine has been thoroughly excavated
And I flood the well-dug mine while you faint biting my tongue and
    flooding my left hand

The circumstances surrounding this exchange make it even more astonishing. Not only was there a gulf in age, sexual experience and worldly sophistication – something that clearly continued to give Madeleine concerns about Apollinaire's motives and intentions – the war caused real practical problems.[23] Letters from Algeria to the front and vice versa typically took a week to arrive, meaning that the lovers' conversation was constantly out of alignment.[24] His letters were written hastily, in a war zone, on whatever paper he could find and sent unrevised. She was able to scrutinize every word at leisure to find nuances that perhaps did not exist, to discover causes for alarm.

So misunderstandings there inevitably were. On 30 July the poet dispatched a long letter explaining the background to some of his most important poems and giving a somewhat skewed account of the love affairs that inspired them. His first love, Annie Playden, 'understood nothing about me'; his pre-war lover, Marie Laurencin, wanted to marry him, but he did not really love her, although he was greatly distressed by the break-up of their affair; Lou remained a great friend but would always be a plaything in men's hands. Almost immediately he regretted sending the letter, and on 1 August he wrote to Madeleine to assure her that he was not a libertine but 'a good and honest lad, whose life only appears to be dissipated'. Her response was to pick on the word *fantasque*, which the poet had used in the earlier letter and which she took in the sense of bizarre, capricious or changeable. He had used it only in relation to the imagination, he had to explain. In mid-August she was shocked to find that her name had appeared in *Case d'armons*, while later in the month she accused him of writing with indifference. Apollinaire, meanwhile, complained shortly afterwards that her letters were too brief, that there was something 'not Madeleine' about her most recent note and that he wanted a 'long letter from my real Madeleine, whom I love, and not from the one who rebels and makes judgements'. He was particularly upset by her failure to comment on his early book of short stories, *L'Hérésiarque et Cie.*, which he interpreted as a sign that she disliked one of his favourite works. 'Perhaps it isn't a book for women,' he suggested.[25]

How then did the couple negotiate these obstacles and find an epistolary *modus vivendi*? With a great deal of persistence, cajoling, encouragement and flattery on his part (mixed with some tact and an occasional element of verbal brutality) and with shyness, reserve but a growing willingness to participate in this intimate exchange on hers.[26]

The letters in late August 1915 are uxorious in many respects, as one might expect given their very recent betrothal. Apollinaire was careful to set the correspondence within the framework of marital duty, doubtless as a way of reassuring Madeleine but also, one feels, a reflection of sincerely held beliefs.[27] Within marriage, he argued, duty – expressed in terms of fidelity and honesty – provides 'that security that allows love to flower and renew itself', turning vice into virtue and 'Hell into Paradise'. Indeed, it is incumbent on the partners to explore the furthest reaches of their sexuality and to be open about their desires in order to avoid satiety and ensure a long and healthy relationship. How many marriages have been unhappy, he asked Madeleine, 'because of a taciturn or over-prudish wife who didn't dare to state her preferences and how she wanted to be loved'? She should prepare for physical as well as spiritual love, he wrote elsewhere, telling him not only her tastes, her dreams and her preferences but the caresses her thoughts had suggested to her. Their separation from each other, he suggested, should allow them to explore the peaks of Platonic love.

While Apollinaire set out his ideas on marital duty the couple also shared views on children, and the poet pictured them as a 'model couple', although he was already enjoining his new partner to leave behind all coyness. The language is respectful, the first use of *tu* only coming on 23 August and then only in the single phrase '*je t'aime*'. It was some weeks before Apollinaire switched fully to this more intimate form of address. But continuing to imagine her body from the photographs she sent, the poet now encouraged Madeleine to provide her own descriptions, and she responded, although only about her eyes at this stage. At the same time, now that they were engaged, Apollinaire made it quite clear how he wanted their correspondence to develop and offered a frank acknowledgement of his intense sexual desire for her. 'Now that we are truly united, my darling,' he wrote, 'we can write freely, and what can I say about the immense desire I have for your young flesh. I'm like an ogre who is presented a little child to eat.'

It is no surprise, given his correspondence with Lou, that Apollinaire saw himself playing a very dominant role in the partnership with his new love. As early as 14 July, so before their betrothal, he had written, 'Your obedience in respect of me must remain complete.' A few weeks later he told Madeleine, 'You MUST NOT doubt me. I take responsibility for your total happiness. No woman will have [a life] as perfect as yours.' And, once again, there was an undercurrent of sexual violence. My desire will take you with 'an infinitely gentle violence, the brutality of an angel', he would write later, while advising her not to fear 'conjugal correction [spanking]' as a painful punishment when, on the contrary, it is 'an exquisite refinement when you love each other as we do'.

September raised the temperature. On the 13th Apollinaire thanked Madeleine for describing her breasts, having encouraged her on the previous day to write about her unspoken desires. He reassured her about her sexual transition into womanhood in poetic images: 'The lily will become rose, and this metamorphosis shouldn't worry you, my love.' Secrecy became an increasingly important theme – 'One is lubricious when one isn't secret about one's love affairs,' he wrote on 18 September – and they spoke of the rich and secret language they were creating together. He continued to express his sexual desires in ever more graphic images ('I grow stiff in your direction as the needle of the compass veers towards north') but at the same time acknowledged her 'exquisite reserve'. He would assume the role of educator in the manner of de Sade, initiating her into 'the natural things that young girls do not generally know about' and creating what he would later call 'a well-informed virgin'.

By 21 September Madeleine was beginning to participate actively in the 'the most charming sport there is', and Apollinaire was writing of the birth of sensual pleasure (*volupté*) in her. 'You have a genius for love,' he told her and included with his letter the first of a series of 'secret poems', a free-verse meditation on the nine doors to her body, from which the following extract is taken:

> Left nostril of my love fifth door of my love and our desires
> I will enter through this into my love's body
> Subtle I will enter with my male scent
> The scent of my desire
> The acrid manly perfume that will intoxicate Madeleine[28]

The poem concludes with the triumphant invocation:

> O doors open to the sound of my voice
> I am the master of the Key

As further evidence of Madeleine's growing contribution to the exchange, on 8 October the poet thanked her for having agreed in one of her letters that they should broaden the scope of their intimate conversations since 'it's our secret marital life that is beginning'. On the following day he encouraged her once again to become less modest, citing the example of 'the admirable passion that beats immodestly' in the works of a great saint such as St Teresa of Avila. 'Yet another effort, my slave!' he exclaims, and two more secret poems are sent as encouragement. A week later he asked for more details about her body. 'But I don't know the colour of your body, whether you see your veins, the shade of your dear nipples. I don't know if everything is as dark as your hair . . . Tell me about yourself, be proud of your beauty.' A fourth secret poem, once again in free verse, expressed his burning desire for her through a series of religious and military images:

> My mouth will have the fires of Gehenna
> My mouth will be an inferno of sweetness for you
> The angels of my mouth will reign over your heart
> My mouth will be crucified
> And your mouth will be the horizontal beam of the cross
> And what mouth will be the vertical beam of that cross
> Oh my love's vertical mouth
> The soldiers of my mouth will storm your womb
> The priests of my mouth will cense your beauty in its temple
> Your body will shake like a region struck by an earthquake

Your eyes will be filled then with all the love that has accumulated in
    human eyes since the beginning of time
My love my mouth will be an army against you
A raggle-taggle army
As multiform as a wizard who knows how to vary his transformations
Because my mouth also targets your hearing and above all
My mouth will tell you of my love
It murmurs it from afar
And a thousand angelic ranks are busy there preparing heavenly
    sweetness for you
And my mouth is Order too that makes you my slave
And gives me your mouth Madeleine
I take your mouth Madeleine[29]

And as October shaded into early November the sexual
content of Apollinaire's letters became ever more ecstatic and
explicit. He imagined undressing her and kissing her eighth door.
He mused on how he would bend her forwards so that her
'marvellous dimpled and fleshy bottom' stuck out, and he would
take her 'like a stallion takes a mare'. And he described the erotic
effects of her letters on him. 'When I read your letters, which are
so voluptuous, an exquisite shudder runs through my whole body,
the sensation concentrates in the same place as in you, but which
is so different to yours, it swells, extends and stands up and begs,
takes off its hat and bends forward in your honour and towards
you.' Meanwhile, the sequence of secret poems continued.

If there is something disturbing about this epistolary seduction
of a naïve young admirer by a worldly author we need to
remember that the repetitive, almost aggressive and obsessive
sexual content of Apollinaire's letters was doubtless an accurate
reflection of the isolation, monotony and sexual frustration felt by
all front-line soldiers. While many British poets found an escape

from the war in pastoralism Apollinaire found solace in eroticism.[30] As he wrote to Madeleine on 11 October, 'Your dear sensuality is a consolation for all the boredom, is the only remedy for boredom.' The poet took full advantage of his skilful pen and, in Lou and then Madeleine, correspondents who were willing to participate in – or at least tolerate – an exchange of such intimacy.

And, as always with Apollinaire, there was a creative and literary element in everything he did. Madeleine was in many respects a fantasy created by words – in Claude Debon's memorable phrase, he is her 'architect'.[31] The poet's idealization of her, the ever more extravagant images he deployed to describe her body and their future sexual relations, the secret language they devised were all ways of meeting his need to create and to produce poetry in the midst of the banality, chaos and horror of a soldier's life in a war zone. Apollinaire himself hinted at this in several poems, calling his beloved 'my dear work of art' in 'À Madeleine' ('To Madeleine') and in 'Plainte' ('Complaint') wondering:

Do you exist my Madeleine
Or are you just a being I've created without wishing to
In order to populate my solitude
Are you like one of those goddesses the Greeks created to combat their
    boredom

The poem concludes: 'But you do exist oh Madeleine your beauty is real', but we are not fully convinced.

As for the young woman herself, she was clearly entranced by this great literary romance, if somewhat taken aback by the speed at which it developed and the direction it took.[32] At twenty-two she felt ready for her first sexual experience, and, once the barriers of modesty came down, she plied the poet with concerns and questions to which he responded patiently.[33] Would they have sex in different positions and with their eyes open? – Yes, they would. Would her first experience hurt? – Not necessarily, as her hymen might already be broken. Was post-coital sadness inevitable? – It was not something he had ever experienced. Nor should the literary element on her side of the correspondence be under-estimated. She was, after all, a young woman who had considered going to acting school (she was dissuaded by her mother, advice of which Apollinaire approved), helped to teach literature in a school and was an avid reader of poetry. How better to develop her own writing skills than in an unbridled correspondence with a leading poet and writer?[34]

As Apollinaire's correspondence with Madeleine grew ever more intense, communication with Lou almost inevitably declined, particularly as she continued to spend much of her time with Toutou in the Vosges or in pursuit of other unnamed conquests. It did not help that the war left her increasingly anxious. 'Above all, have as little to do with the war as possible,' Apollinaire advised her on 11 July. 'It's all you talk about, it's all you think about. It's absolutely ridiculous to shred your nerves like this.' The poet still enjoyed hearing from her. 'Your long letter delighted me and really excited me,' he wrote on 14 July. He still claimed to love her and continued to express the hope that they would resume their sexual relations. 'I'd really like to try out the new way of spanking that I've invented,' he told her. But one senses that his emotions were no longer fully engaged.

Indeed, several of the poems he sent to her during this period have an air of wistfulness, setting their affair well and truly in the past. In 'Cote 146' ('Hill 146') the poet questions whether he has ever truly known her:

I also look at a portrait of you in a large hat
        And some of my comrades saw your portrait
        And assuming that I knew you well
        They asked
        Who's she then
And I didn't know what to reply to them
        Because I suddenly realized
        That even now I hardly know you[35]

On 1 September he wrote, 'No doubt we'll not meet before the end of the war and who knows when!! And who knows how!! Who knows if we'll even see each other again?', while a letter later in the month contained a short valedictory poem in traditional twelve-syllable alexandrines:

When two noble hearts have truly been in love
Their love is stronger than death itself
Let us gather the memories that we've sown
Absence after all is nothing when you love one other

Other poems took a new, satirical turn. In the fable of 'Les Fleurs rares' ('The Rare Flowers') Apollinaire mocked Lou's incessant bed-hopping. She had already plucked one flower:

But passing through the forest
En route to her train at the next town
    Li'l Lou saw under an oak tree
Another flower It looks even more beautiful
    The first flower tumbles
    And the forest becomes its tomb
While li'l Lou with a dreamy air
    Has plucked the second flower[36]

Apollinaire's mother Angelica in 1899
(© Roger Viollet/Topfoto)

Apollinaire and the artist André Rouveyre in Paris on
1 August 1914 on their return from Deauville
(© Roger Viollet/Topfoto)

Left: Louise de Coligny-Châtillon (Lou) in 1914 (© Roger Viollet/Topfoto)

Below: Apollinaire flanked by comrades at the Champagne front, 1915 (© Roger Viollet/Topfoto)

Left: Yves Blanc, Apollinaire's 'war godmother' (© Roger Viollet/Topfoto)

Below: A sentry in a front-line trench in the Champagne region, 1915–16 (Archives Larousse, Paris/ Giraudon/The Bridgeman Art Library)

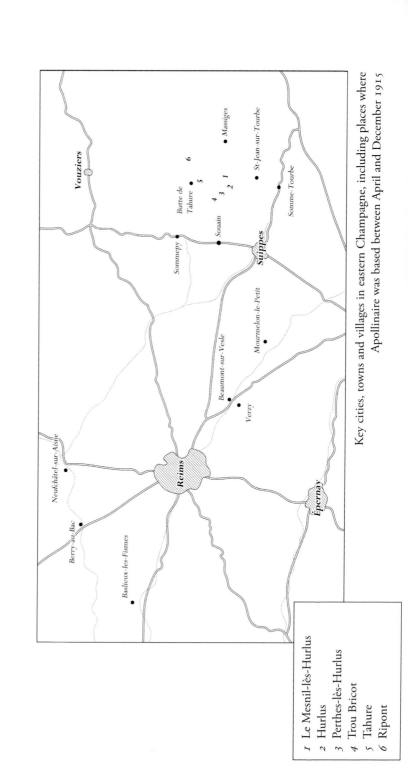

Key cities, towns and villages in eastern Champagne, including places where Apollinaire was based between April and December 1915

1 Le Mesnil-lès-Hurlus
2 Hurlus
3 Perthes-lès-Hurlus
4 Trou Bricot
5 Tahure
6 Ripont

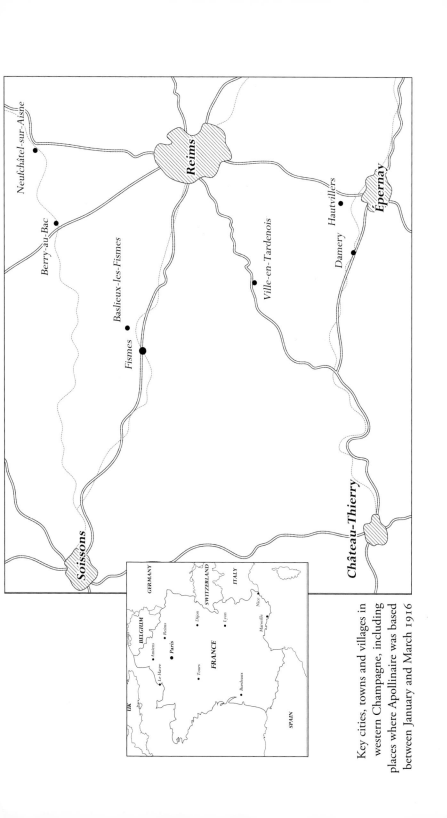

Key cities, towns and villages in western Champagne, including places where Apollinaire was based between January and March 1916

Apollinaire with Madeleine Pagès in Algeria, January 1916 (© Roger Viollet/Topfoto)

Apollinaire drawn by
Picasso, 1916
(© Roger Viollet/Topfoto
© Succession Picasso/DACS,
London, 2014)

Apollinaire at the Conservatoire Renée
Maubel before the première of
Les Mamelles de Tirésias
in Paris, June 1917
(© Roger Viollet/Topfoto)

Apollinaire with his wife Jacqueline at the 'pigeon loft', 202, boulevard Saint-Germain, in 1917 or 1918 (© Roger Viollet/Topfoto)

A second fable, with the punning title of 'Le Toutou et le Gui' ('The Lapdog and the Mistletoe'), offered as a moral 'There's no point trying to understand', reflecting ironically the poet's early statements about army life.

Underpinning Apollinaire's laughter, however, was a note of pity for Lou's chaotic emotional life that had not been heard so clearly before. 'How can you not be happy, but what's up then, in your last letter you told me you were happy, you were the one who underlined the word,' he wrote on 24 September, calling her 'my poor little Lou always scalded by love'.

Increasingly, then, she was the one who was chasing him for letters and sending photographs. As early as July he had told her, 'I prefer to respond to the letters that you send me.' 'I don't know why you were so het up,' he wrote a fortnight later. 'You didn't write, I didn't write. Perhaps it's stupid, but it's a wonderfully mnemonic method. You receive a letter, you respond to it; there you are.' During the following months she continued to complain about the lack of letters, but the poet was no longer willing to play the game. So when, on 9 November, Apollinaire started a letter with 'My dear Lou, a fortnight! It's at least a month since you wrote to me. I congratulate you on being in love and on leading such an interesting life' it almost sounded like a valediction. As, indeed, it proved – only four further short letters to Lou survive.

There was another reason for Apollinaire's cooler relationships with Lou. In the late summer of 1915 he acquired a 'war godmother' (*marraine de guerre*).

In his Nîmes barracks the poet had a reputation for devising witty quatrains to celebrate the departure of comrades for the front. When he himself set out in April 1915 his colleague Émile Léonard asked a young family friend, the poet and novelist Jeanne

Burgues Brun, who wrote under the male pseudonym of Yves Blanc, to provide a similar send-off. Her deliberately archaic quatrain reached Apollinaire in August 1915.

> You are going to accomplish the valiant deed
> Of Polish heroes on our forefathers' soil
> Bear with you the dark fates to defy
> This hope-filled quatrain from a woman of France

On 16 August Apollinaire responded with his own short poem, mirroring Yves Blanc's alexandrines, and a correspondence was born.[37]

During 1915 a number of voluntary associations and newspapers had promoted the idea of linking soldiers at the front with 'godmothers' who would help to sustain the troops' morale as well as sending packages and gifts. Particularly in the more lurid parts of the popular press, however, the godmothers quickly acquired a reputation for straying well beyond their initial brief. Apollinaire's first letter to Yves Blanc therefore adopted an inappropriately flirtatious tone, addressing her as 'the little girl that you are' and making reference to the 'sadness that we should be able to console' that he claimed to sense in her. Yves was having none of this. Despite repeated requests from Apollinaire she refused to send him a photograph, to describe her features or to talk of her personal life.[38] The correspondence is thus of particular interest for what it tells us about the poet's aesthetic ideas and ambitions and how he saw the contemporary literary landscape. If the comments in Apollinaire's letters to Yves, Madeleine and a small number of other literary correspondents are combined, what emerges?

First, that poetry was everything. As Apollinaire wrote to Madeleine on 11 August, 'Life is only painful for those who keep themselves distant from poetry through which it is true that we are in the likeness of God. Poetry is (even etymologically) creation. Creation, the serene expression of intelligence outside time, is the perfect joy.'

Second, although Apollinaire wanted to be a new poet 'as much in form as in content', he retained a tremendous admiration for the great classical authors such as Racine, unlike 'some modern writers who are not grounded in their art', as he told Yves Blanc. La Fontaine and Rabelais, he said to the writer Willy in a later letter, are perhaps the most characteristically French authors. Gautier is an 'exquisite poet'; Banville is 'charming' and an important influence on poetic practice. Foreign authors are cited approvingly – Shakespeare, Cervantes and Tolstoy ('a sort of Jupiter of the novel') but also Whitman, Twain, even Goethe.[39] Overall, though, Apollinaire expresses a preference for authors who achieve a balance between psychological and realistic detail and who incorporate an element of humour into their work. 'I don't like it when you look at the defects, vices or deformities of mankind without smiling, which is a way of understanding and remedying our misery to some extent by cloaking it in intelligent gracefulness, even if we were to sob later.' The charming, laughing Gogol is therefore his favourite Russian author.

On the other hand a lot of contemporary literature left Apollinaire cold.[40] D'Annunzio was 'really false'. Pierre Louÿs 'an artificial writer, a real but narrow talent' (although *Les Chansons de Bilitis* was a long-shot that came off). Colette's work was characterized by 'lots of affectation, little naturalness and a boarding-school talent, a surface sensitivity'. Claudel is Rimbaud as small change, a penny coin to Rimbaud's golden sovereign: 'He hasn't had the courage to move outside himself and above all to go beyond the literature of images that is so facile today.' Meanwhile, the poet Verhaeren and his ilk are 'pretty flat', but their opponents offer nothing but 'vague and really uncertain traditionalist or classical principles'.

To admire the classics, then, was not to be mired in outdated conventions, which are a sort of coyness. Art must be beyond good taste. 'Do you see a Tolstoy, a Dostoyevsky, a Balzac or a Zola or, even more so, a Rabelais limiting themselves to writing poetry with a rhyming dictionary?' he asked Yves in November 1915. He himself wanted to be part of no school and he had no poetic system – or, rather, he had many.[41]

The best way to be classical and weighty, he advised Yves, was to be 'of one's time without sacrificing anything that the Ancients had been able to teach us'. There could not be authentic lyricism nowadays, he said later, without the poet having complete freedom, even if he then chose to write regular verse. He himself, he wrote to Madeleine on 3 August, composed his poetry by singing. 'Once a musician even wrote down the three or four tunes which I use instinctively and which are the manifestation of the rhythm of my existence.'

And his best work? From his 1913 collection *Alcools*, he told Madeleine, he particularly liked 'Vendémiaire' and 'Le Voyageur' ('The Traveller'), but 'the newest and the most lyrical, the most profound' was 'Fiançailles' ('Betrothal'), which with 'Le Brasier' ('The Inferno') he felt was his best poem if not his most immediately accessible. As to the future, he makes clear his view in several letters to Yves that his *idéogrammes* (later to be named *calligrammes*) were the most innovative part of his pre-war work and 'the newest thing I've invented in relation to the art of poetry'. They reflected important poetic needs and were so new, he claimed, that they had anticipated practices that had now become common. 'Since the beginning of the war topography has been "ideogrammatized" and communiqués from the front constantly bring you the names of enemy or French constructions baptized after their shape: the trapeze, the trident, the dagger.'[42] Apollinaire was proud to have been in the vanguard of these linguistic developments.

6
CHAMPAGNE
NOVEMBER 1915–MARCH 1916

'My dearest love, I haven't written to you for two days. Called upon to become an officer. I couldn't refuse.' On 24 November 1915, and in this rather abrupt fashion, Apollinaire announced to Madeleine a major change in his military status. Henceforth he would be a second lieutenant in the 6th Company of the 96th Infantry Regiment in command of a platoon of around fifty men – almost certainly the most dangerous rank in the army.[1]

The letter was less than truthful. The poet himself had requested the move, which had finally been approved on 18 November. Nor was this a sudden decision. As early as July 1915 Apollinaire had begun asking André Level to investigate the process by which an NCO in the artillery might become a junior infantry officer. Level declared himself 'astonished' and tried in vain to dissuade his friend from considering the change. Just at the point where Apollinaire's competence as an artilleryman was established he wanted to learn another task. Level admitted to being thoroughly perplexed.[2] But he sought out the information none the less, and his reply on 28 July to the effect that Apollinaire would have to petition the commanding general through the normal channels suggests that Apollinaire must have submitted his transfer request well before November.

What were the poet's motives for making a move that he would clearly have known to involve much greater danger and discomfort?[3] In purely practical terms, officers were better paid, travelled first class on trains and avoided the menial tasks that were the bane of a non-commissioned soldier's life. But Apollinaire's letters make little of this. To Madeleine he invoked the desire to pre-empt on his own terms a transfer that was likely to happen in any case, given the army's need to replace infantry casualties. 'There will certainly be some ranks in the art. that will go into the infantry, and perhaps not immediately as officers. And can you see me as a sergeant in the infant.?' What was more, a lucky wound might end his war and put him in a place of safety. At the very least, his longed-for leave would be brought forward.

However, the move was also entirely consistent with the ambition Apollinaire had displayed from the earliest days of his military service. 'My military career would only begin to shine if I became an officer and was really able to do something,' he told one correspondent.[4] Accepting a commission in the most dangerous part of the army would not just bring him the advancement he sought but would make him worthy of respect and even love. In a telling phrase in a letter of 24 November the poet told Madeleine that 'a love like ours demands a very great sacrifice'. Later he would write that 'perhaps a wound is required for me, too, if I'm to become worthy and pure for you'.

Life in the artillery did not demand enough of a sacrifice. The letters from Apollinaire's early weeks in the infantry are peppered with unfavourable comparisons between the two services, almost to the point of suggesting that gunners were effectively incompetent shirkers.[5] An NCO in the artillery lived much more comfortably than a senior officer in the infantry, where the attitude was different – much more gallant. Serving in the artillery was like a walk in the park, hardly more risky than mountain-climbing, 'bourgeois messing' (*popote bourgeoise*). Infantrymen were serious, never coarse and highly disciplined; gunners quite the opposite. The artillery was 'a service for grandfathers and eunuchs', he told Lou in one of his last letters to her.[6]

That these remarks were unfair, to say the least, was brought home by an encounter between the poet and his former artillery comrades on 20 December. On a march forward he found his battery in an advanced position, a dangerous spot where there was no shelter for the guns. In an emotional exchange he discovered that almost all his gun crew had been 'massacred or wounded', including his master gunner from Lille, Louis Déportère, a young man whose wife and baby were still in the occupied zone.[7] 'I don't remember anything more about it, I was so upset by the other losses,' he wrote to Madeleine, adding that if he had stayed with the battery he would have been wounded at the very least. There were few further remarks about the artillery's easy life.

But there was always more to these comments than mere crass inter-service rivalry. Apollinaire clearly felt that the experience of the front-line infantryman was the closest he could get to the essence of the war, the depths of which as a poet he wished to sound. 'At last, at last, at last real trench life,' he wrote to Madeleine on 29 November. The letters speak of the 'the naked and profoundly fated drama of front-line war' and of the infantry being 'the only interesting and formidably tragic service'. Even the landscape and *matériel* of the front had their own extraordinary allure. 'Then there's the mystery of trenches caught in enfilading fire . . . the mystery of barbed-wire spheres, listening posts, saps, the noises we hear, of the unexpected names given to different points on the secret map.' No writer will be able to describe 'the simple horror, the mysteries of trench life', he wrote to Madeleine from a position opposite the German lines. For a poet, what could present a greater challenge?

In fact Apollinaire's time in the infantry is notable for how few poems he produced, certainly in comparison with his period in the artillery. The reasons are not hard to find. During November and December 1915 he completed two tours of duty in the front-line trenches of the Hurlus area, an initial nine days (extended to eleven) from 28 November and then a further period from 18 to 23 December.[8] A letter to Madeleine on 29 November (which the regimental war diary records as a day when the troops were up to their knees in water or mud) gives a vivid description of the rigours involved even in reaching the front line in this most desolate of landscapes: the pep-talk delivered by the battalion commander; the evening departure across icy ground on which 'the soldiers slipped and fell like flies'; the pale, flayed plain stretching out in front; 'the infinitely zigzagging communication trenches that lead to the front line'.[9] Even for a soldier with Apollinaire's length of service this was to be a new and terrifying experience.

Once in position, and living like 'real Troglodytes', the troops faced 'nine days without washing, sleeping on the floor, without straw, on ground full of vermin'. Simply maintaining the chalk trenches in winter conditions required unremitting effort. As Apollinaire wrote to André Level on 3 December, 'The thaw makes these atrocious trenches collapse. We work night and day to repair them and the myth of Sisyphus repeats itself 20 or 30 times here in 24 hrs. The mud is excessive.'[10] Securing the defences against German attack also involved hard physical labour, particularly if the company previously holding that part of the line had not been sufficiently assiduous. 'As our predecessors hadn't done anything,' Apollinaire wrote about his second tour of duty in late December, 'there's everything still to do. I spent the night getting barbed-wire spheres made, getting them thrown out in front, making new battlements, installing chevaux-de-frise.'

All of this work took place in conditions where what would normally be considered horrific had become routine – Apollinaire noted that a parapet in his trench was partly built from corpses, and he could clearly see bodies hanging on the barbed wire in no-man's-land[11] – where the poor weather conditions and difficulties of replenishment meant that hot food and even drinking water often became luxuries, where everyone from the most senior officers down was infested with vermin and where danger was ever present.[12] Particularly terrifying, as Apollinaire explained to Madeleine, were the different types of trench artillery – nicknamed variously howlers, shit boxes, coal scuttles and Marie-Louises – in the development of which the Germans had made rapid progress.[13] But this part of the line was also subject to ferocious bombardments and gunfire. 'The theatre itself can't give you an idea of the terrible bombardment that suddenly colours the sky purple, of the whistling of the shells as they pass through the air like cars passing on the ground during a race, of the tearing explosions of the shells and torpedoes, of the mad crackling of gunfire dominated by the tac tac tac of machine guns close by.'[14]

Little wonder then that the troops talked only of war, the Germans and the daily round of deaths and woundings. Nor that one of only two poems that Apollinaire sent to Madeleine during his initial few weeks in the front line, the free-verse 'La Tranchée' ('The Trench'), presents the trench as a sexually alluring, bewitching and bloodthirsty femme fatale, as this extract suggests:

I am the white trench with the hollow white body
And I inhabit all the devastated earth
Come with me my lad into my vulva which is my whole body
Come with me penetrate me and delight me with bloody voluptuousness
I will heal your sorrows your worries your desires your melancholy
With the fine clear song of bullets and the orchestra of artillery
See how white I am whiter than the whitest bodies
Lie on my bosom as in a beloved womb
I want to give you a matchless sleepless wordless love
I have loved so many young men

I love them as Morgan Le Fay does
In her castle whence none return
On the heights of Mont Gibel

As a junior officer Apollinaire's responsibilities included three two-hour periods of trench duty in every twenty-four hours. The poet described this routine as 'annoying but very necessary'. Where men might not sleep properly for days on end, an important function for an officer was to keep sentries awake, shaking them or even threatening them with a court-martial. Life for an infantry officer was hardly bearable; for the ordinary soldier it was much worse. Apollinaire therefore had immense sympathy for the young men ('these poor children') under his command. 'They're good men, devoted and full of courage,' he wrote to Madeleine on 9 December, while a week earlier he had noted, 'The country will never have enough admiration for these simple infantrymen, admirable soldiers who die gloriously like flies.'[15]

The poet himself seems to have been a good officer, allowing his sergeants to share his dug-out and his men to warm themselves at his brazier and to heat up their broth on his fire. 'My men like me a lot,' he claimed, 'because I'm jolly, I don't stick in my dug-out, I go and see them, encourage them, find out how they are eating.' At the same time one can catch glimpses in the letters of the grievances that would contribute to the mutinies in the French Army in 1917: the frustration that senior officers seemed to understand so little about life on the front line ('they never come to see the trenches'); the lack of relaxation even when the troops were out of the line ('rest that's hardly restful at all and can be cancelled from one minute to the next'); the horrible facilities provided in the rear areas, even for officers.

*

If Apollinaire produced few poems during November and December 1915 he did continue to write almost daily to Madeleine, even from the front-line trenches. Not surprisingly the letters dwelt on his new life in the infantry and the landscape of the front. But he also responded to Madeleine's stories about Algeria, reassured her that he would not volunteer for any dangerous missions and dealt with practicalities – on 30 November, for instance, dispatching two parcels containing catalogues and pieces of clothing.

At the same time the erotic content of the letters remained high. Madeleine was by now writing the sort of letter (what the poet calls 'lettre-volupté') that he had always sought. 'It's extraordinary how well you write, my darling, and with what skill you can talk about everything with tact and with an admirable sense of voluptuousness and of my needs,' he told her on 26 November. 'Your progress in us is exquisite,' he said later in the same letter. With his encouragement she continued to explore her body and to describe it for him: 'What you tell me about the little hermit makes me madly happy,' Apollinaire wrote. 'I adore it when it's hard. That's the one. You've found it, my dearest love.'[16] She was also inventing erotic games, exchanging epistolary embraces ('I adore your caresses at my ninth door,' he exclaims) and negotiating the terms of their future sexual relations. 'Yes, you're right, nudity for us: we'll keep our clothes on only during outdoor adventures,' Apollinaire agreed in early December.

Confronted more than ever by the true horrors of the front line, Apollinaire responded ecstatically to the flowering of Madeleine's sexual imagination.[17] A secret poem sent on 7 December described the 'symphonic song of love' that sounded in her mount of Venus:

This is what makes up the symphonic song of love that sounds in Venus's conch
There's the love song of bygone times
The sound of illustrious lovers' wild kisses

The love cries of mortal women raped by the gods

The virile members of mythic heroes erect like church candles go back
    and forth like an obscene murmur

There are also the mad cries of the Bacchantes maddened with love after
    eating the hippomanes secreted by the vulvas of mares in heat

The love cries of big cats in the jungle

The muffled murmur of sap rising in tropical plants

The roaring of tides

The artilleries' thunder when the cannon's obscene shape consummates
    the terrible love between peoples

The waves of the sea where life and beauty are born

And the victorious song that the sun's first rays made motionless
    Memnon sing

There's the cry of the Sabines at the moment of their rape

The bridal song of the Sulamite

I am beautiful but black

And Jason's propitious yell

When he found the fleece

And the dying song of the swan when its down pressed itself between
    Leda's blue-tinged thighs

There is the song of all the love in the world

Between your darling thighs

Madeleine

The murmur of all love just as the sea's sacred song sounds complete in
    the seashell[18]

While he continued to imagine new details of their love-
making, Apollinaire increasingly set Madeleine on a pedestal as
the ultimate object of desire. 'I feel you are as abandoned as Leda,
wise as Helen, passionate like Sappho, learned like Héloïse,
charming like Agnès Sorel, ardent like Catherine the Great.'
Through her letters and her love she also acted as a talisman, a

guardian angel hovering above the atrocities of the front line. 'My love,' he told her, 'in the mysterious metallic horror which is mute but not silent . . . our love is the only star, a perfumed angel that floats above the yellow and black smoke of the exploding bombs.' Even their past became myth, their initial meeting a thunderbolt where her beauty completed 'that marvellous capture of my heart which was yours in the blink of an eye'. When they exchanged addresses, Apollinaire tells her, it seemed to him that they were exchanging their souls.

'If you knew how much I desire you at the moment', the poet wrote to Madeleine on 14 December. The point where those desires might be consummated was now approaching. Earlier in the month Apollinaire had submitted a leave request to his colonel, giving his reasons for wanting to travel to Algeria. By 5 December he was able to tell Madeleine that his commander had accepted his arguments (it helped that the colonel was a former colonial soldier) and that he was now third in line for a break. On 18 December he was advised to be ready to depart on the 23rd, although Apollinaire warned Madeleine that the arrangements were never definite. But he did eventually leave the war zone on the evening of 22 December, arriving in Marseilles on the 25th and embarking for Oran on the 29th. The couple would now come face to face with the images they had created of each other.

No one knows quite what took place between the fiancés during Apollinaire's ten-day leave in Algeria, and it remains one of the great unexplained mysteries of the poet's life. There are some photographs of the couple standing rather awkwardly together, and a short article by Apollinaire that appeared in April 1916 – 'L'Histoire du permissionnaire' ('The Story of the Man on Leave') – mentions some of the local sights, but the poet's letters and his subsequent poetry and fiction give away little of substance. More recently a memoir of the poet's visit, written by Madeleine and retained in the family archives, has been published.[19] However, the account was written some thirty years after the event and paints a very contented – perhaps idealized – picture of the couple's time together. Certainly, there is no hint of future storms.

In principle, Madeleine had committed herself to fulfilling all the poet's desires: 'Your dear promise intoxicates me. I'll be your rock during my leave. All the doors will belong to me you say. What a happy doorman I will be during my leave,' he wrote on 5 December. In practice the presence of a large family and a watchful mother must have limited the opportunities – Madeleine's memoir makes clear that the couple were constantly chaperoned. In any case, could the meeting ever have lived up to the expectations placed upon it? Madeleine was, after all, a young teaching assistant living in a French colony far from both sophisticated Paris and the war zone, while Apollinaire was a leading member of the avant-garde who had now spent nine months at the front and had experienced in the weeks leading up to his leave the full horrors of trench warfare. Even soldiers who had been married many years found it difficult to communicate to their families what they were going through.

Whatever the reasons, Apollinaire's letters to Madeleine from the time he returned to the war zone in early January were markedly different in tone from those he had previously sent. They were shorter, devoid of any real sexual content, more functional in every respect. The change was not immediately apparent. A note sent from Marseilles on 10 January 1916 thanked Madeleine, her mother and all the family for 'the delightful leave you afforded me'. Two days later Apollinaire wrote to say he had informed his mother, Angelica, about his betrothal, and she had no objections. He mused on Madeleine's beauty, sweetness, imagination and looks. On the 17th he assured her that he was 'going to see about marriage by proxy', meanwhile telling Ardengo Soffici, editor of *La Voce*, that Algeria and Oran had been 'amazing'.

But by the third week in January Madeleine had sensed a cooling off and was expressing concern. 'No, there's no separation in spirit from you,' Apollinaire wrote on the 25th; he would deal with their marriage as soon as he had a moment. Madeleine remained unconvinced, and Apollinaire's comments during late January and the early part of February reflect her increasing panic: 'I want you to calm down' (29 January); 'I'll deal with our marriage as soon as I know what I have to do about it' (3 February); 'Don't worry about the brevity of my letters . . . Don't expect anything very loving at the moment' (10 February); 'I want you to be stronger, my love, and not to create phantoms for yourself' (13 February); 'Don't get hysterical, keep calm, I beg you' (14 February). It did not help that the post to Algeria seemed to be suffering from major delays.

Apollinaire's explanation for the change in his letters was simple. He was too exhausted to write at length and, in addition, a tougher censorship regime inhibited him from repeating his earlier effusions.[20] On his return from Algeria he had rejoined his regiment at rest in Damery, south-west of Reims. He was asked to take temporary command of his company and was immediately assailed on all sides by rear-area bureaucracy and interference.[21] 'Report after report,' he wrote to Madeleine on 15 January. 'Yesterday even the general wanted to know why the sentry on some road or other didn't have a lamp.' He was beginning to miss the front line, he added; at least there you were pestered only by the Germans.

There then began a period when Apollinaire and his comrades were constantly overworked and on the move, often in very difficult wintry conditions.[22] On 22 January they left Damery to begin full-scale manoeuvres at Ville-en-Tardenois. A move to Hautvillers followed on 4 February; on 22 February they reached Fismes and on 6 March took up positions nearby in Baslieux-les-Fismes. The poet later characterized his life during this period as being like a gypsy's. 'I'm living in a dream. It feels as if I've been dragging my feet in the mud on the main roads for an eternity. I'm becoming an automaton, unable to think.'

'Stupefied by all this work', 'burnt out', 'disoriented in this precarious life as an infantryman' are some of the ways in which Apollinaire described himself during these months. There were some bright spots – he was 'indescribably moved' by leading out his company at the head of the regiment on a route march, and there was a memorable visit to Reims, 'a city both dead and alive', where he saw shop girls serving impassively in a big department store while shells fell around them. His mood was still good, he would tell the writer Paul Léautaud on 21 February, but in the same letter he admitted that he was prone to 'sudden violent outbursts that no longer surprise the friends who know me well'.[23] A bout of influenza in that same month left him in a state of deep melancholy.[24]

He began to look for ways out of his current posting. In the middle of January Apollinaire discovered that new machine-gun units were being formed.[25] However, he had not been nominated for a position because his colonel wanted to familiarize him with the life of the infantryman first. Undeterred, he immediately asked Level to search out and send him a machine-gun officer's manual, which arrived by late January. Apollinaire's ambition was never realized, but the very fact that he contemplated such a move so soon after joining the infantry indicates the enormous impact these first experiences of trench warfare had on him.

*

'Remember how many poems I wrote in the art.', Apollinaire complained in early February, 'and how many have I written in the infant., perhaps not one.'[26] In fact, he did produce a few poems in the early part of 1916, including one of the most ambitious and complex of all his war poems, 'Du coton dans les oreilles' ('Cotton in Your Ears'), which he began to sketch out surreptitiously during a lecture on gas on 10 February and a rough draft of which was sent to Madeleine on the following day.

Apollinaire had been thinking about this work from at least the end of January when he announced to Madeleine that 'I'd also like to start a long poem on the war', adding that this would be 'the first song (*chant*) of my new work'. And the finished poem is extraordinary in a number of ways. The first section alone surprises in the unusual layout of the words on the page and the combination of typefaces and fonts, suggesting the noise and impact of shellfire. The complete work mixes references to life at the front, including the poet's own journey from the artillery to the infantry, *calligrammes*, songs, audacious images and puns, as well as different metres and voices (introducing elements of the 'conversation-poems' found elsewhere in Apollinaire's output). It creates an almost delirious bombardment of noise that leads eventually to an equally menacing silence in the final lines, the likely prelude to an enemy attack that may involve gas.[27]

One other feature of this period stands out: the poet's burgeoning correspondence with the young poet and future surrealist André Breton.[28] Breton had approached Apollinaire in late 1915, sending him copies of his own verse and seeking his help in tracking down Apollinaire's publications, including *Case d'armons*. A conversation about the arts ensued. A couple of letters from February 1916 offer fascinating insights into Apollinaire's literary tastes and principles. He claims to read mainly 'specialist books on every subject' and to be familiar with chivalric and obscene

COTTON IN YOUR EARS
(FIRST SECTION)

So many explosives just about to be

ALIVE!

d a^r^e   *war*

you   *at*

if   *continually*

word   *soul*

a single   *my*

Write   *in*   fire

of impact   out

points   spits

The   flock

fierce

Your

OMEGAPHONE

?

works but devotes little time to modern novels. He does not doubt the importance of Mallarmé but finds him overly Parnassian, just as Valéry is too refined. Rimbaud, on the other hand, 'foresaw many modern things' and his corpus is 'small but so powerful'. As for his own work Apollinaire justifies the 'broken form' of some of his poems as a way of rendering the infinite variety of life. 'I'm not an aesthete. I pursue my own tastes. They are simple and not always refined,' he claims, adding that sometimes 'to go far, you have initially to return to first principles'.

On 14 March 1916 Apollinaire heard that his naturalization as a French citizen had been formally announced five days earlier.[29] That same day his company was one of several sent forward into the front line near the Bois des Buttes, north-west of Reims, in an area described by the regimental war diary as consisting of 'flooded communication trenches, small in number, major works on 1st and 2nd lines'. The position was extremely precarious and exposed to enemy fire. 'Didn't sleep all night,' he wrote to Madeleine on the 15th. 'No description possible. It's unimaginable.'[30]

He was reading a copy of the *Mercure de France* during a period of calm when the shell landed around 4.00 p.m. on 17 March. A piece of shrapnel pierced his helmet just above the right temple, splattering the pages with blood. Gravely wounded, according to regimental records, he was given a preliminary dressing at the regimental aid post before being evacuated under heavy shellfire to Field Hospital (*Ambulance*) 1/55 at Romain near Fismes where he underwent an operation during the night to remove the fragments of shell. 'In the event', he told Madeleine in a military card sent on the 18th, 'the helmet saved my life.'[31] By the 20th he was at the main hospital (*Hôtel-Dieu*) at Château-Thierry, where the records noted 'a scratch on the cranium'. A further operation was planned for the following day, but on 22 March Apollinaire was able to tell Madeleine that radiography had shown there was no need to repeat the surgery carried out at the field hospital.[32]

Although Apollinaire downplayed the severity of his wound in his cards and letters to Madeleine he was clearly in poor condition. He could barely write, and most of the early correspondence after being wounded is dictated. Anti-tetanus injections were causing him much pain. And fever delayed his evacuation to Paris, which eventually took place only on 28 March when he began the move to Val-de-Grâce hospital, arriving the following day. On 9 April a further transfer took him to the Italian Government Hospital, an annexe of Val-de-Grâce located at 41, quai d'Orsay where there were fewer patients and his friend, Serge Férat, was a nurse. But despite the excellent care he received his health continued to decline over the following month – 'I've been forbidden to go out because I've had some accidents like fainting fits and trouble with my left side, my left hand above all,' he told Madeleine on 1 May – and the need for further surgery became increasingly evident. On 9 May, at the Villa Molière annexe, he was trepanned to allow for the removal of a haematoma caused by his wound, an operation judged successful. As yet unable to write, he began to spend much of his time painting in pastel and watercolour.[33] A regimental citation on 17 June awarding him the Croix de Guerre stated that he had given 'in every circumstance an example of sang-froid and courage'. But this brave soldier, who had none the less remained a poet, would never see active service again.

And what became of Madeleine? In the weeks immediately following his wounding Apollinaire was assiduous in sending her regular, if brief, summaries of his progress. 'Head wounds heal quickly,' he reassured her. There are cards or letters from the 18, 19,

21, 22, 24, 25, 27, 28 and 30 March. But longer gaps began to appear in April, and he also refused to allow the young woman to visit him in Paris, despite her obvious concern and emotional distress. 'I can't live like this,' she wrote in the early summer, describing herself in the same letter as panic-stricken and deeply unhappy.[34] He discouraged her from contacting him. 'Don't send me telegrams that upset me too much,' he wrote on 1 May. Apollinaire pleaded disgust with Parisian life, sadness at the death of comrades, overwhelming fatigue and the need to avoid the strain of writing – no doubt with justification in view of his condition. But the emotional distancing that Madeleine had sensed in January was now fully apparent. By mid-May the correspondence had virtually ground to a halt on his side, and the few surviving letters of any substance from Apollinaire thereafter are mainly concerned with retrieving his notebooks and other objects that Madeleine was holding in safe-keeping. No letters from him exist for the period after November 1916. Just as the shell had shattered Apollinaire's life as a front-line soldier, so it sounded the death knell on his already waning love affair with Madeleine.

7
PARIS
APRIL 1916–NOVEMBER 1918

The final two years of Apollinaire's life were punctuated by bouts of serious ill health. 'I'm not the man I was in any respect,' his final letter to Madeleine declared, and as regards his physical constitution he was right. 'The trepanning continues to have a profound effect on me,' he told Ardengo Soffici, in early August 1916. 'I still haven't managed to get back to work.'[1] A fortnight earlier he had warned Yves Blanc that he would need at least a year to recover fully from trauma of the head wound that had nearly killed him.

He had been allowed to return home to his flat at 202, boulevard Saint-Germain during July 1916 but was kept under close observation by his doctors and required daily treatment at Val-de-Grâce hospital until the early months of the following year. As late as November 1916 he was complaining to Soffici that his left arm was 'still inert' and required 'a great effort of will to make it move'.[2] In that same month he felt unable to read some of his poems at a poetry matinée, and Cocteau had to step in as reciter.

The effects of his head wound were intensified by other medical problems. Although he had boasted of his iron constitution in letters to friends such as Level, Apollinaire acknowledged from early on the inevitable deterioration in his health that life at the front would bring. In August 1915 he had spoken to Madeleine of his 'marvellous health that the war is weakening and will weaken yet more'. Shortly afterwards he wrote to her, only partly in jest: 'I'm afraid the peace will return you a gout-ridden suitor, crippled with pain.'

To the damage caused by cold and damp was added that of gas. The protection offered to French soldiers in the early part of the war remained rudimentary and their improvised solutions less than effective: 'You use your scarf against gas shells, you wet it, and there you go,' he told Lou within weeks of arriving at the front. The after-effects were profound, leaving him vulnerable to chest complaints and leading to a further two-month period of hospitalization at the Villa Molière in early 1918 for congestion of the lungs followed by almost three months of convalescence. 'I was a hair's-breadth from dying,' he wrote of this episode.[3] The army acknowledged the severity of his health problems by declaring him unfit for further service (*inapte définitif*) on 11 May 1917, effectively absolving him from any future front-line duties, although he remained part of the military establishment.

Apollinaire had something of a reputation for touchiness before the war, and ill health left him in an even more sombre and fractious mood. 'I'm still very tense, excessively irascible,' he told Yves Blanc soon after his return to Paris. 'It's extraordinary how I'm tired of everything, even of life itself, dare I say. I'm in a very difficult period in terms of morale,' he wrote to Soffici.[4] The wider progress of the war did not help to boost spirits. Throughout the spring and summer of 1916 the French and German armies bled themselves dry at Verdun, while on 1 July the British–French assault on the Somme began with its attendant slaughter. Meanwhile in August 1916 Romania declared war on the Austro-Hungarian Empire, but initial attacks were quickly driven back, and Austrian and German troops entered Bucharest on 6 December. Towards the end of the year morale in the French Army fell to its lowest level since the retreats of 1914, and political criticism of the High Command grew increasingly vocal, leaving

Paris awash with rumours and intrigue. On a personal level, too, the poet was suffering. 'My comrades are almost all dead,' he told Madeleine in September 1916. He hardly dared write to his colonel for details. His friend André Dupont had been killed, as had Berthier's brother. Apollinaire's wound had allowed him to escape the inferno, but the war could still reach him.

All of which may help to explain, at least in part, the tensions in Apollinaire's personal relationships, particularly with his mother Angelica.[5] The two had frequently been at odds in the past: 'strained relations and must take good care between mother and me', he had warned Lou in April 1915. A letter to Madeleine in September of the same year was more explicit. 'She is indomitable, completely indomitable as only Slav women can be (read Dostoyevsky), and I can only be myself when I'm away from her; when I'm near she always treats me as if I were ten years old . . . she loves me too much, and I love her just as much.'

Apollinaire would claim in August 1916 that, despite his wound and his return to Paris, he had not seen his mother since mid-April of that year and that he was no longer writing either to her or his brother Albert in Mexico. Relations seem to have been re-established by early 1917, but by March 1918 Apollinaire was telling Toussaint Luca, 'Mother is fine, but I'm on bad terms with her. Her very demanding nature has caused a temporary rift between us.'

Comments in Apollinaire's correspondence with Madeleine give a clue as to why relations with Angelica should again have been tense. 'She'll always be jealous of anyone her son loves,' he had warned her. And by spring of 1918 Apollinaire was not only in the middle of a new love affair, he was planning to marry.

Amélia Emma Louise Kolb, known as Jacqueline, or Ruby because of her red hair, had been the girlfriend of the poet Jules-Gérard Jordens, who was killed at the Bois des Buttes in April

1916. She probably already knew Apollinaire by then, but their affair only began in earnest towards the end of the year. On 31 December she accompanied him to a banquet given in his honour by friends and admirers and attended by around a hundred guests. By early 1917 Apollinaire's friends were appending greetings to Ruby to their correspondence, and there was even the suggestion in a letter sent by Apollinaire to Picasso on 22 March 1917 that she was pregnant (her postscript to his letter says 'the first heir is on the way!!!!!'). However, no child was born. The couple were married on 2 May 1918 at the Town Hall of Paris's 7th Arrondissement and at the Church of Saint-Thomas d'Aquin, with Picasso acting as one of the witnesses.[6]

Jacqueline was an inspiration for one of Apollinaire's most famous poems, 'La Jolie rousse' ('The Pretty Redhead'). In the following extract her hair is compared to the sun, and the poet's new love is linked to a renewed ardour for poetic creation:

Summer is coming the violent season
And my youth is dead as is spring
Oh Sun it is time for ardent Reason
   And before I follow her
For ever I'm waiting for the noble and sweet form
She'll put on so that I love her and her only
She comes and attracts me as a magnet attracts iron
  She comes in the shape
  Of an adorable redhead

Her hair is made of gold one might say
A gorgeous flash of lightning that lasts
Or flames dancing
In tea roses fading[7]

In spite of this homage, Apollinaire's relationship with his new wife seems to have had little of the devastating passion of his previous liaisons.[8] In his late thirties, weakened by his time at the front and his wound, anxious about his finances and keen to re-establish himself in Paris, the poet was seeking a more stable, if perhaps more prosaic, framework for his life.

Although now deemed unfit for active service Apollinaire had volunteered for the duration of the war and was therefore still officially part of the army establishment. When treatment for his wound came to an end he was assigned, on 20 June 1917, to the press-relations section of the Ministry of War as a censor. For someone who had sought ways of coding his letters from the front line and who at one point had written to Madeleine that 'in my view the suppression of the press would have been more adroit than its censorship' there was a certain irony in the new position.[9] A later posting, in May 1918, would take him to the Ministry for the Colonies, where he edited a bulletin that brought together articles in the foreign press relating to colonial affairs.

Alongside his official duties Apollinaire also accepted a range of other, often onerous, journalistic jobs in order to supplement his still meagre army pay – translating foreign dispatches from 6 a.m. onwards for the journal *Paris-Midi* between January and April 1917, for instance, and fulfilling a similar early-morning role for the stock-market journal *L'Information* in April 1918. The poet complained to friends that he was left with little time and energy for his own work.[10] Nevertheless, fatigue, ill health and his military duties notwithstanding, Apollinaire remained remarkably productive in the period after his return from the front.

In late October 1916 a collection of short stories, *Le Poète assassiné* (*The Murdered Poet*), was published. The tale that gives the volume its title and which occupies almost half the book chronicles the life of the poet Croniamantal from his conception through to his violent death, Orpheus-like, at the hands of a hostile crowd. Earlier in the year Apollinaire had written to Madeleine that the story was 'an attempt at a more lyrical story with an element of satire'. Autobiographical allusions – both Picasso and Marie Laurencin appear as barely disguised characters – are mixed with references to myth. Playful, at times vulgar, language combines with an overall tone of sadness. In terms of the conventions of the realist novel favoured at this point in the war (the Goncourt jury awarded a double prize in 1916 to Barbusse's *Le Feu* and Adrien Bertrand's *L'Appel du sol*) *Le Poète assassiné* was badly constructed and written. However, Apollinaire was attempting something different – to escape from the conventions of realism and psychological analysis and to find a path between prose and poetry in a work with its own internal coherence.[11]

Although most of the stories in *Le Poète assassiné* were written before the war Apollinaire added a final story to the volume before its publication, 'Le Cas du brigadier masqué c'est-à-dire le poète ressuscité' ('The Case of the Masked Corporal, That Is, the Resuscitated Poet'), in which the poet, like a 'new Lazarus', leaves his cemetery and joins the army.[12] There he meets a strange masked corporal who sets before him a vision of the war that both draws on and distorts Apollinaire's own experience: 'In large expanses of snow and blood he [the poet] lives the hard life of the front; the splendour of the exploding shells; the watchful gaze of the exhausted sentries; the nurse giving the wounded man something to drink; the artillery sergeant who's a runner for an infantry colonel awaiting with impatience his girlfriend's letter; the platoon leader doing his rounds in the snow-covered night.' Characters from the other stories in the volume reappear in this final tale in their wartime guises, as does Apollinaire's friend René Dalize under his own name. The story ends with the masked corporal suffering a head wound from which emerges 'a triumphant Minerva', and the final sentence urges, 'Stand up, everyone, to give a courteous welcome to victory!'

If *Le Poète assassiné* challenged contemporary conventions of realism, Apollinaire's next major work, *Les Mamelles de Tirésias* (*The Breasts of Tiresias*), turned them on their head.[13] In a preface to the published version of the play he claimed that in order to characterize his drama he had been obliged to create a new adjective, surrealist, signifying something more real than reality.[14] As he explained, 'I thought it necessary to come back to nature itself, but without imitating it in the manner of photographers. When mankind wanted to imitate walking he created the wheel, which does not resemble a leg. He therefore brought about surrealism without knowing it.'

The play was premièred on 24 June 1917 at the Conservatoire Renée-Maubel in Montmartre. Apart from Louise Marion, who played Tirésias, the cast was made up of mainly unknown and (given wartime conditions) under-rehearsed actors. The drama caused an immediate brouhaha. 'I've just scandalized Paris,' Apollinaire wrote proudly to one correspondent, although he was less happy when a group of artists, including 'Metzinger, Gris and other arseholes like that', sent an open protest to the press in the name of cubism.[15] Indeed, there could have been serious consequences for Apollinaire's position in Paris – for a time he was concerned that his superior at the Ministry of War might take fright over the commotion and send him off to train new recruits and convalescents at his regiment's base at Béziers in the south of France.

In the drama Thérèse leaves her authoritarian husband and

adopts the masculine identity of Tirésias in order to pursue positions of military, political and social power. Her husband, meanwhile, allows the feminine side of his nature to flourish and in one miraculous day gives birth to 40,049 children. This main story is intertwined with a series of secondary narratives involving characters such as two duellists, a mounted policeman and an American journalist. There are songs, music and other background noises produced by musicians, a male voice choir and the 'People of Zanzibar'. Towards the end of the play a mysterious fortune-teller appears, who turns out to be none other than Thérèse herself, determined now to rejoin her husband and to produce even more children. In the closing dialogue Thérèse stresses the importance of love:

> What matters the throne or the tomb
> We must love one another or I succumb
> Before this curtain falls

Although Apollinaire claimed in his preface that most of the play dated from 1903, the contemporary references in the text would have been very apparent to the audience on the opening night. Concerns over the size of France's population, particularly in relation to a unified and resurgent Germany, had been expressed before 1914 but became especially acute during the war as French manhood was expended on the battlefield.[16] In the free-verse prologue that opens the drama – the section of the play most admired at the time – the director of the troop of actors addresses the audience directly, painting a picture of a night at the front:

> One evening when in the sky the eyes of the stars
> Quivered like the eyes of newborn children

Enemy artillerymen are now firing so high that they are extinguishing the stars themselves, one by one. But French gunners are their equal:

> The gunners hurried
> The aimers aimed
> The firers fired
> And the sublime stars reignited one after another
> Our shells stoked their eternal flames

The director makes clear the morale of the story: the need to repopulate earth with new generations of French men and women:

> And let the land everywhere be studded with infants' eyes
> More numerous even than the twinkling of stars
>
> Hear oh you French the lesson of the war
> And create children you who had scarcely created any

Repopulation was not the only concern threaded through the text. The year 1917 had opened in a burst of renewed optimism. Germany's decision to issue a 'Peace Note' in early December of the previous year had been interpreted by many as a sign of weakness, while the breaking off of diplomatic relations between the USA and Germany in February 1917, following the latter's resumption of unrestricted submarine warfare, raised hopes that France might acquire a powerful new ally. General Robert Nivelle had replaced Joffre as Commander-in-Chief of the French armies on the Western Front, promising a more aggressive pursuit of the war.

Sadly, any hopes that the war might soon end proved to be empty. Nivelle's Chemin des Dames offensive, launched on 16 April 1917, saw some 147,000 Frenchmen killed, wounded, missing or captured in the space of a fortnight. In response to this new and apparently pointless massacre, and to the harsh conditions under which French soldiers continued to fight, a rash of mutinies broke out in the army, peaking in the period between 20 May and 10 June. Meanwhile, a bitter winter (the Seine was ice-bound in February 1917) combined with food shortages caused by German submarine warfare brought renewed hardship to the home front, and over the same period France was rocked by a massive outbreak of strikes, twenty-four on 30 May 1917 alone, mobilizing more than 50,000 workers.

What particularly shocked people at the time was that these strikes were mostly led by women, who had replaced the absent menfolk in factories (including the war industries), in some parts of the public and service sectors and even, in some cases, as drivers in the army.[17] While the 1915 strikes in Glasgow – also largely organized by women – had been mainly concerned with rents, the protesters in France (where the government had acted early in the war to control rents) called for better pay and working conditions. In both Britain and France, however, the demonstrations were coupled with increasing demands for universal suffrage. Thérèse, then, is in many ways the model of a modern woman, and the play's focus on the fragility of marriage and the difficulties of male–female relationships mirrored the concerns that men at the front had about their wives and girlfriends.

In fact, Apollinaire had long been interested in the role and status of women, in part for political and social reasons but also because of questions of sexual identity. Frustrated with the apparent failures of French diplomacy he had written to André Level in September 1915 that 'women will henceforth be more important in France than men, if we entrust diplomacy to them it will be done well and certainly better than now', mirroring similar comments elsewhere in his letters.[18] But his views were often contradictory, combining an at times almost Utopian belief in women's social and sexual freedom with the authoritarian tendencies of a man with a powerful male self-image in a deeply misogynistic period.[19] Thérèse returns to her husband, therefore, to fulfil her reproductive destiny, but both husband and wife have changed by the end of the play: the husband is more joyful, less authoritarian, more broad-minded; Thérèse is calmer and less intransigent but no less vivacious.[20]

If the subject matter of *Les Mamelles* is serious the treatment is not.[21] In his prologue the director promises the audience that the actors 'will concern themselves above all with amusing you', and Apollinaire draws on a wide range of popular theatrical influences – music hall, circus, pantomime, boulevard drama, Guignol – and exploits as many visual, auditory and linguistic resources as he can (including, for instance, an exotic setting in Zanzibar) in order to create a work that is a joyous affirmation of creativity and artistic fecundity. The dramatist himself is at the heart of the play, as the prologue announces:

> His universe is his play
> Within which he is god the creator
> Who disposes at his will
> Sounds gestures action masses colours
> Not with the sole intent
> Of photographing what is called a slice of life
> But to make life itself leap out in all its truthfulness

In short, as Peter Read has commented, in a time of sadness and austerity Apollinaire reclaims the right to liberty, joy and pleasure.[22]

*

The most important work of Apollinaire's war years appeared the following year, in April 1918: *Calligrammes: Poèmes de la paix et de la guerre (1913–1916).*[23] This volume of poetry was dedicated to the memory of Apollinaire's oldest friend René Dalize, who had died at the front on 7 May 1917, and it had had a long and complex gestation, with many poems going through multiple versions before their eventual appearance in the book.

In the period leading up to the war Apollinaire had been working on an album of 'lyrical and tinted idéogrammes' (*idéogrammes lyriques et coloriés*) under the title *Et moi aussi je suis peintre (And I Too Am a Painter).*[24] The album was incomplete in August 1914, and the project was never realized. On his return to Paris in 1916 Apollinaire initially envisaged publishing a book of his war poems, but eventually the *Mercure de France* was persuaded to produce a more ambitious volume that would also include a number of Apollinaire's works from the pre-war period, including some originally destined for the album abandoned in 1914. During the spring of 1917 subscription bulletins announced the forthcoming appearance of *Calligrammes* (the word now replaced *idéogrammes*), but a combination of wartime restrictions on materials, the lack of skilled publishing staff in Paris as a result of mobilization and the complexities of realizing the poet's vision for his calligrammes on paper all contributed to delays. It was not until the end of 1917 that a more or less complete dummy was ready, and the collection appeared the following April. In the meantime Apollinaire had published some of the individual poems in small literary magazines.

The process had been long, and Apollinaire had had constantly to modify his intentions in the light of wartime conditions. However, he took advantage of the delays to clarify and enrich his original conception. Even the change to the dates in the subtitle, from the original 1913–1917 to the final 1913–1916, had a poetic significance, since some of the poems do, in fact, date from 1917. The volume is about the poet's personal experience and journey in the period leading up to and during the war, culminating in the head wound in 1916 that ended his direct involvement.

The poet's journey is reflected in both the content and the structure of the collection. Most of the verse was composed contemporaneously, and unlike Apollinaire's other main collection, *Alcools*, published in 1913, few of the poems incorporate fragments from the poet's youthful sketches, underlining the plenitude of new images and inspiration that the war had offered. Again unlike *Alcools* the main sections of the volume follow a broadly chronological pattern linked to the poet's life, although with important exceptions.

The first section, 'Ondes' ('Waves'), groups together a variety of pre-war poems, including 'Les Fenêtres' ('Windows'), which was originally published in the catalogue for Robert Delaunay's exhibition of paintings in Berlin in January 1913, and the visually complex calligramme 'Lettre-Océan' ('Ocean-Letter'). Meanwhile, in the visionary free-verse 'Le Musicien de Saint-Merry' ('The Musician of Saint-Merry'), an enigmatic ambulant musician – like the Pied Piper or perhaps Orpheus – draws behind him a crowd of women from history, literature, mythology and the poet's own past life.[25] The following is an extract:

> Processions oh processions
> The women so great was their number
> Overflowed into all the neighbouring streets
> And rushed on stiff as chaff
> Following behind the musician
> Ah! Ariadne and you Paquette and you Amine
> And you Mia and you Simone and you Mavise
> And you Colette and you the lovely Genevieve
> They passed by trembling and vain

And their light swift steps followed the cadence
Of the pastoral music that guided
Their eager ears

The stranger stopped for a moment before a house for sale
An abandoned house
With broken windows
It's a dwelling from the sixteenth century
The courtyard serves as a garage for delivery lorries
There the musician entered
His music became languorous as it grew distant
The women followed him into the abandoned house
And all of them entered in a jumbled mass
All all entered without a backward look
Without regretting what they left behind
What they abandoned
Without regretting the day life or memory
Soon there was no one left in La Verrerie Street
Except myself and a Saint-Merry priest
We went into the old house
But we found no one there

The next section of the collection, 'Étendards' ('Standards')
spans the declaration of war ('La Petite auto' – 'The Little Auto'),
the poet's meeting with Lou ('La Mandoline l'œillet et le bamboo'
– 'Mandolin Carnation and Bamboo'), his imminent departure
for the front ('Veille' – 'Night Watch') and his estrangement from
his lover ('C'est Lou qu'on la nommait' – Lou They Called Her).
However, the penultimate poem, 'Ombre' ('Shadow'), was almost
certainly written later and, full of distress and pity, offers a sombre
reminder of the bitter realities of war and the way in which it
haunted ex-combatants:

Here you are at my side again
Memories of my companions dead at war
Olive of time
Memories now all sewn into one
As a hundred furs make only one coat
As the thousands of wounds make only one newspaper article
Impalpable and sombre apparition grown
To the shifting shape of my shadow
An Indian on the lookout for all eternity
Shadow you crawl along beside me
But you no longer hear me
Nor will you know the divine poems I sing
While I hear you I see you still
Destinies
Multiple shadow may the sun watch over you
You who love me so you never will go away
Who dance in the sun without kicking up dust
Ink shadow of the sun
Script of my light
Caisson of regrets
A god who humbles himself[26]

There follows 'Case d'armons' ('Limber Store'), which incorporates the poems of Apollinaire's June 1915 publication but presents them in a different order and with some amendments. This, in turn, is followed by 'Lueurs des tirs' ('Gun Flashes'), which brings together a series of poems that, with one exception, were sent to Madeleine in the late summer and autumn of 1915. However, the first seven poems of this section were, in fact, composed for a charitable project being undertaken by the poet's pre-war lover Marie Laurencin and dispatched to her in Spain via their mutual friend Louise Faure-Favier. Poems such as 'Les Feux

du bivouac' ('Bivouac Fires') combine regret for a lost love with
an underlying bitterness at the rupture:

> The bivouac fires flickering
> Illuminate the forms of dream
> And in the interlacing
> Branches reveries gleam
>
> Here are the disdains of regret
> Galling as a strawberry
> The memory and the secret
> Whose embers only remain[27]

In five of the remaining eight poems in this section Madeleine
is evoked, while the final poem, 'Océan de terre' ('Ocean of
Earth'), develops a comparison found in a number of contemporary accounts between the undulating landscape of Champagne,
the rolling noise of shellfire and a seascape as well as possibly
offering a description of a gas attack:

> I've built myself a house in the middle of the ocean
> Its windows are the rivers that flow from my eyes
> Its walls are crawling with octopuses
> Listen to their triple hearts beat and their beaks rap at the panes
>> Dank house
>> Ardent house
>> Brief season
>> Song season
> The airplanes are laying eggs
> Watch out we're going to drop our inkers
> Watch out for the ink we splot
> It would be good if you came down from the sky

Sky's honeysuckle is twisting up
Earth's octopuses pulse
Besides so many so many of us dig our own graves
Pale pulp of the chalky waves oh octopuses your pale beaks
All around my house there's this ocean as you know
That never rests[28]

Any notion of strict chronology breaks down at this point, as the period of composition of many of the poems in the penultimate section of *Calligrammes*, 'Obus couleur de lune' ('Moon-Coloured Shells'), overlaps with that of the previous section. As well as giving a final version of 'Du coton dans les oreilles' ('Cotton in the Ears'), written in February 1916, this part of the collection contains one of Apollinaire's great kaleidoscopic enumeration poems, 'Il y a' ('There's'), with its mix of immediate experience, memory and imagination:

There's a ship that sailed away with my love
There are six sausages in the sky and at nightfall you'd think they were
    maggots giving birth to the stars
There's an enemy submarine out of sorts with my love
There are thousands of little pine trees broken by the shells that are
    bursting shells all around me
There's an infantryman going by blinded by gas
There's that we've diced the tripe of Nietzsche Goethe and Cologne
There's that I long for a letter that hasn't come
There are in my wallet several photos of my love
There are prisoners going by with anxious faces
There's a battery whose gunners bustle around the guns
There's the post orderly coming jogging along Lone Tree Road
There is they say a spy prowling round invisible as the horizon he's
    brazenly put on and into which he blends
There's my love's bust sitting tall as a lily

There's a captain who's anxiously expecting news from the Atlantic on
  the TSF
There are soldiers at midnight sawing planks for coffins
There are women screaming for corn in front of a bloody Christ in Mexico
There's the Gulf Stream which is so warm and so good for us
There's a cemetery full of crosses 5 kilometres away
There are crosses everywhere you look
There are Barbary figs on those cactuses in Algeria
There are my love's long graceful hands
There's an inkwell I made in a flare 15 centimetres long which they
  wouldn't send off
There's my saddle left out in the rain
There are the rivers that don't return to their sources
There is love that bears me gently along
There was a Boche prisoner carrying his machine gun on his back
There are men in the world who've never been to war
There are some Hindus who look with astonishment at our Western
  countrysides
They think sadly of those they are wondering if they will ever see again
For the art of invisibility has made great strides in this war[29]

The final section of the collection, 'La Tête étoilée' ('The Star-
Studded Head'), completes the overturning of chronology by
mixing poems written after Apollinaire's posting to the infantry
with some written earlier and three composed after he was
wounded. The section contains the rather grandiloquent 'Chant de
l'Honneur' ('Honour's Song') in which poet, trench, bullets and
France engage in a debate, the poet arguing that beauty alone can
counterbalance death:

> But here as elsewhere this I know beauty
> Is most of the time no more than simplicity

And how many have I seen dead in the trenches
Who had remained standing with their heads bowed
Leaning simply against the parapet[30]

Most of the poems in this part of the collection still have the figure of Madeleine in the background, but the final two turn towards Jacqueline Kolb. 'La Jolie rousse' ('The Pretty Redhead'), which ends the book, as well as paying homage to the poet's new wife sets out a prospectus for new worlds yet to be conquered by poetry, which his death soon after turned into a testament. The following extracts can be seen as reflecting contemporary debates about the future of poetry, which set traditionalists against a younger generation for whom the war had tainted anything smacking of the past:

I stand before you all a sensible man
Conversant with life and whatever the living can know of death
Having experienced the pain and joy of love
Having now and then convinced others of his opinions
Knowing several languages
Having travelled a good deal
Having seen war in the Artillery and the Infantry
Shot in the head chloroformed and trepanned
Having lost his best friends in the terrible fight
I know as much about the ancient and the modern as any man
And setting aside today my concern about this war
Between us and for us my friends
I'm going to judge the long quarrel concerning tradition and invention
      Concerning Order and Adventure

. . .

We are not your enemies
We want to offer you some vast and strange domains
Where mystery holds out its flower to whoever would pick it
There are new fires colours never before seen
A thousand imponderable fantasies
To be made real

We want to explore this bounty a huge country where everything is silent
There's time as well that we can get rid of or bring back
Have pity on us who are forever skirmishing on the borders
Of the boundless and the future
Pity for our errors pity for our sins[31]

Rejecting both a hidebound attachment to convention and a rootless search for novelty, Apollinaire would continue to argue fiercely and consistently for embracing the best of both the old and the new, most notably in his paper on the future of poetry, which was first delivered as a lecture by the actor Pierre Bertin in late November 1917 (Apollinaire once again being ill) and subsequently published under the title *L'Esprit nouveau et les poètes* (*The New Spirit and the Poets*).[32]

Apollinaire described *Calligrammes* as a war book (*livre de guerre*) and argued that it would therefore touch people much more than his previous volume *Alcools*.[33] While increasingly a focus for study by literary specialists the collection has largely been ignored as a document by historians, perhaps because of its modernity. But there is a tremendous amount that can be learned about the soldiers' lives, their slang and superstitions, the conditions in which they fought and the horrors they faced, whether gas or barbed wire.[34] 'Le Palais du tonnerre' ('The Thunder's Palace'), for instance, offers a vivid picture of a dug-out and trench very similar to the ones Apollinaire himself had inhabited, although the details are, as always, integrated into a poetic response to the surroundings in which the poet finds himself. The poem begins:

Looking through the opening to the trench carved out of the chalk
Towards the far wall that looks as if it were made of nougat
One can see to left and right dank deserted passageways fleeing
And a shovel dying flat on its back with its frightful face and the two eyes
    used to fix it to the caissons
A rat backs off as quickly as I advance
And the trench goes on and on vaulted with chalk strewn with branches
Like a hollow ghost leaving behind itself a ghastly emptiness
And overhead the roof is blue and stretches well over the view barred by a
    few straight lines
But on this side of the opening there's a brand-new palace that looks old
The roof is made of railway ties
Between them are lumps of chalk and clumps of fir needles
And now and then a piece of chalk breaks off and drops like bits of old age
Next to the opening closed by a flap of a kind of fabric used for packing
Is a hole that serves as a hearth and what is burning there is a fire that
    resembles the soul
Because of how it swirls up and how fleeting and inseparable it is from
    whatever it devours[35]

Against this background of life at the front Apollinaire pursues a number of themes throughout the volume. Love, of course, appears in a variety of guises, prompting poems that range from celebrations to elegies, all of them drawing extensively on images of the battlefield. There are at least ten poems in the volume that can be linked directly to the person of Madeleine, who, in the absence of any physical contact with the poet, becomes, it can be argued, a largely allegorical figure representing the beloved awaiting the return of her soldier-lover.[36] But, as we have seen, Marie Laurencin is also present. Sadly, Lou's presence is much attenuated, and it remains unclear whether the poet was unable to recover the poems he had sent to her or whether he chose not to use them.[37]

Some of the poems have been criticized for veering towards propaganda, and there are certainly lines in 'À l'Italie' ('To Italy') and '2ᵉ Canonnier Conducteur' ('Artillery Driver Second Class') that now appear crude – 'Hear the braying of the Hun donkey', for instance.[38] Such poems are few in number, however. More important is the underlying sense of fraternity in the collection, which can embrace the poet's comrades, the men serving under him when he becomes an officer and humanity itself, including perhaps the enemy combatants. The inclusion of fragments of ribald soldiers' choruses and the use of poetic forms that suggest folk songs evoke a specific French community; but one of the most famous poems in the volume, 'Les Soupirs du servant de Dakar' ('The Sighs of the Dakar Gunner'), is a sympathetic and subversive imagining, unique for its time, of the experience of one of France's many colonial soldiers who fought and suffered terribly at the front. The poem begins:

> In the dugout of logs behind a screen of willows
> Next to grey cannons pointed north
> I am dreaming of the African village
> Where we danced where we sang where we made love
> And long speeches
> Noble and joyous

It ends:

I am a French soldier you might say I've been whitened
Sector 59 I can't say where or
What makes being white better than being black
Why not dance and make speeches
Eat and then sleep
And we shoot at the Boche supply lines
Or at the barbed wire in front of the squaddies
In this blizzard of metal
I remember a horrible lake
And couples chained together by an atrocious love
A crazy night
A night of witchcraft
Like tonight
Where so many horrible gazes
Explode in the resplendent sky[39]

A further criticism sometimes made of the collection, particularly in the post-war years, was that it glorified a war that had proved to be an unparalleled catastrophe for the peoples of all the belligerent nations. 'Merveille de la guerre' ('Wonder of War'), for example, starts:

How beautiful these flares are that light up the night
They climb to their own peaks and lean out to gawk
They are ladies who dance with their glances for eyes arms and hearts

It is certainly true that Apollinaire found new inspiration and images in his involvement in the war and the word *merveille* has overtones of medieval mysteries, fairy stories and chivalric romances.[40] But this same poem also evokes the bloodthirstiness of the trenches and the fires burning human flesh. Rather than taking the pity of the war as his focus, as Wilfred Owen famously did,

Apollinaire's ambition therefore seems wider: to capture all the extraordinary aspects, all the highs and lows, all the different perspectives, all the resonances of a conflict that he and his contemporaries recognized would be, for good or ill, the defining experience of their lives. As a stanza later in the same poem suggests:

> I leave to the future the story of Guillaume Apollinaire
> Who went to war and knew how to be everywhere
> In the happy cities behind the lines
> In the whole rest of the universe
> In those who die walking into coils of barbed wire
> In the women in the cannons in the horses
> At the zenith at the nadir of the 4 cardinal points
> And in the particular ardour of this night's watch[41]

Meanwhile, Apollinaire's lyricism is often underpinned by sharp sense of irony that commentators have not always fully recognized.[42] The 'mad laughter behind the mask' in a poem such as the 'Chant de l'horizon en Champagne' ('Song of the Horizon in Champagne') not only evokes the absurdity of life at the front but the physical effects of a gas attack and the hysteria such weapons induced. The much-debated 'L'Adieu du cavalier' ('The Horseman's Farewell'), in which moments of wartime tranquillity counterpoint the cavalryman's inevitable and possibly unlamented death, should likewise be read in this spirit rather than as a facile glorification of war's amusements:

> Lord! How pretty war is
> With its songs its free time
> See this ring I have polished
> The wind grasps at your sighs

Farewell! The trumpet sounds for me
He disappeared round a bend
And died up there while she
Laughed at what fate can send[43]

In terms of verse form the poems in *Calligrammes* can be broadly categorized into those that encourage a visual scanning before they are read, those in free verse and those in regular verse. However, many poems are a mixture of all three types, and the same verse form is seldom used twice, meaning that there are few 'pure' poems in the collection. Regular verse becomes more common as the reader moves through the volume, but even here the poems may not rhyme in traditional ways.

Within this framework the poet combines and juxtaposes references to the present and the past, to a multitude of places, to his experience of the war and his love affairs, to myths, songs and folk tales. There are snatches of conversation, phrases taken from posters or leaflets, syntactic liberties and ruptures, complex word plays.[44] Different registers, the comic and the serious, rhyme, assonance and echo, the typeset and the apparently handwritten all intermingle. In the face of such fragmentation and discontinuity (which, Apollinaire would have argued, reflected life itself and his experience of modern war) the poet's creative mind and presence, expressed through language, becomes the main – perhaps the sole – point of coherence in the collection, and the reader is invited to follow that mind in all its divagations.[45]

The volume received a mixed reception. Most critics paid homage to Apollinaire's service as a soldier, and a number complimented him on managing to create new forms, sounds and colours from the misery of the trenches. Others, including his friend André Billy, found the collection puzzling and harked back to the more traditional lyricism of the poet's previous collection, *Alcools*. The *calligrammes* in particular were seen by detractors as largely incomprehensible fantasies (not helped by their being printed on paper of very poor quality). Yet Apollinaire had long been interested in typography – *Alcools* combines roman and italic typefaces – and for him the *calligramme* represented an evolution from the codified structures of traditional poetry towards poetic forms that were more appropriate to a new era. His writings show him sensitive to how traditional verse forms exploited layout on the page in ways that had perhaps become invisible to readers. To one critic of his early experiments he responded, 'With my *idéogrammes* [*calligrammes*] I've tried to find a form that, without being free verse, didn't fall back into so-called classical verse. My images have the value of a line of verse. They have a fixed typographical or lapidary form (just like not only the line of verse but the stanza, the sonnet, the rondeau, etc.).'[46]

The *calligramme*, then, was not simply a way of communicating the shape of an object but a means of establishing a whole new set of relationships between different elements of a poem, including the text and the image. It was a carefully considered multiplication of possibilities, not a simplistic search for novelty.[47] The war did not dry up the poet's thirst for ever-new truths, it stimulated and fed that thirst. Apollinaire's reinvention of poetic form would inspire later generations of young artists, not just in France but worldwide.[48]

The final major work that Apollinaire completed after his return to Paris was the drama *Couleur du temps* (*Colour of Time*). The contrast with the earlier *Les Mamelles de Tirésias* could hardly be starker. Wit, verbal invention and farce give way to tragic intensity, dialogue in verse and static settings. The play was premièred on

24 November 1918, a fortnight after the poet's death, but he would have seen some of the early rehearsals.

The drama begins in a country threatened by war. Three men, a poet Nyctor, a scientist Ansaldin and a financier Van Diemen, decide to leave in order to find lasting peace elsewhere. Flying over a battlefield they land in order to experience the realities of war and there meet a mother (Madame Giraume) and a betrothed (Mavise), both of whom are grieving over Madame Giraume's dead son.[49] The women join the men on their journey, and the act ends with a chorus of the dead and the living chanting 'Farewell Farewell everything must die'.

The second act takes place on a desert island where the characters debate at length the meaning of their departure. They encounter a man who has gone into voluntary exile in order to atone for a treasonable crime. All leave just as a volcanic eruption engulfs the island. The final act begins with a poetic set piece in twelve-syllable alexandrines in which Nyctor depicts the gods of all eras crying over man's fratricidal nature:

> All the assembled gods weep to see men
> Kill each other under the sun that also weeps

The voyagers reach their destination – the South Pole – but on finding there the body of a woman encased in ice the men fight to possess her and kill each other. Only Madame Giraume and Mavise remain, and the latter laments:

> Here is that peace so beautiful and white
> So motionless and in the end so dead
> Here is that murderous peace
> For which men fight each other
> And for which men die

The play ends with a reprise of the 'Farewell Farewell' chant heard earlier.

The text suggests a darkening of Apollinaire's mood in 1918 and perhaps even a sense of survivor's guilt. The poet had, after all, been seriously ill at the beginning of the year, and his oldest friend, René Dalize, had been killed at the front in May 1917. The play also reflects wartime preoccupations among creative artists about their response to the conflict, which in the case of the Dadaists and surrealists would lead to a vigorous rejection of pre-war artistic norms in the period after 1918, as well as concerns that the regimentation of wartime France would inevitably lead to a conformist, even oppressive, post-war French society.

At the beginning of the second act, for instance, there is a discussion about duty and the individual's relationship to the collective. Should we remain part of a particular nation state or race with its emphasis on false glory, or should we be seeking a new order, perhaps even a universal art beyond current divisions?

> ANSALDIN
> Do you want to be nothing but a slave
> To grand collective words
>
> MAVISE
> But those grand words represent
> Real beings Motherland
> Nationalities or even races
> Of which we are a particle . . .
>
> ANSALDIN
> So be it and yet
> Beyond your States whether civilized or not
> Out of blood a new order is born

> There is born a State a great State
> The nation of those who want
> No more sovereign words no more glory

On a more personal note, later in this same act, Mavise expresses her growing attraction for the poet Nyctor and the duty she now feels to accompany him. But Nyctor is clearly deeply troubled by his decision to flee his country, indeed by his very survival:

> . . . this child Nyctor
> Who keeps himself apart
> Who is ashamed of having left
> Ashamed of being a poet
> Ashamed of being alive

The era in which the characters live is described as 'the twilight of love' by the voices of the dead and the living, while the ultimate irony is that the lasting peace, so passionately sought, can only be achieved by the extinction of men.

For a number of the poet's contemporaries the formal elements of the play were a step backwards from the exuberant and experimental aesthetic of *Les Mamelles*. However, the almost oratorio-like conception of many of the scenes, added to new scenic elements (including probably the first representation of an aeroplane on stage), can be said to represent for Apollinaire a significant step towards a new and modern form of drama.[50]

As 1918 drew to a close, Apollinaire continued to develop new projects and plans, with a holiday in Brittany during August helping to restore his spirits and health. 'The climate must be amazing for the lungs,' he wrote to Serge Férat on the first day of the month. A parodic-comedy (*comédie-parodique*), *Casanova*, based on an episode from Casanova's memoirs, was completed during the break, with music by Henry Defosse, the conductor at the Ballets Russes. Other publications were also in preparation or on the stocks, including a film script *La Bréhatine* (*The Woman from Bréhat*) which was never put into production. Separate sketches on life in Montparnasse during the war and the history of the Mormons in nineteenth-century USA were merged to form the manuscript of *La Femme assise* (*The Seated Woman*), a novel that would eventually be published in 1920 and an early version of which has been described as a masquerade on the deceitfulness of men and the duplicity of women.[51] There was even talk in the poet's letters to Picasso of a set of odes that the painter would illustrate. 'I'm trying to renew poetic tone but in the classical rhythm,' Apollinaire wrote in September 1918. He could do this, he added, because 'I have never abandoned rhythm, which is at the heart of all my poems and forms their framework.' Sadly, no trace remains of these poems.

The end of the war was also in sight. The USA had declared war on Germany in April 1917 and was expected to send some two million men to France in 1918. In order to forestall the defeat that this new influx of Allied manpower would almost inevitably bring, and boosted by the transfer of troops from the Eastern Front following the collapse of the Russian war effort under the Bolsheviks and the signing of the treaty of Brest-Litovsk, the Germans launched a last great series of offensives in France and Belgium from March 1918 onwards. Wilting under the attack, the Western Allies were forced into retreat, and Paris was once again threatened.[52] However, the Germans had exhausted all their resources, and when the Western forces began to counter-attack in July 1918 – large numbers of American troops were now in the line – their army could not hold. By early November, with Austria-

Hungary having signed an armistice and mutinies and civil unrest growing in Germany, it was clear that the war was finally entering its last days.

How poignant then that Apollinaire should have published a short article in the *Mercure de France* in the early autumn of 1918 commending onion juice as a remedy for the Spanish influenza and that André Level's final letter to the poet, sent on 3 November, should say that his wife was also now in the grip of the flu, but he hoped that Apollinaire and Jacqueline had managed to avoid it. He sent both of them his very best wishes in the hope of seeing them again soon. Within a week the poet was dead.

On his gravestone are inscribed three stanzas from his long wartime poem 'Les Collines' ('The Hills'):

> I have detached myself at last
> From all natural things
> I can die but cannot sin
> And what no one has ever touched
> I have touched I have felt
>
> And I have examined what no one
> Can in any way imagine
> And I have weighed many times
> Imponderable life even
> I can die with a smile
>
> Accustom yourself as I have
> To these wonders I announce
> To the kindness that will reign
> To the suffering I endure
> And you will know the future[53]

EPILOGUE

Within months of the end of the war Apollinaire's direct family line was extinguished. His mother, Angelica, died of influenza on 7 March 1919, a few days after her long-term partner Jules Weil had succumbed to the same infection. Apollinaire's only sibling, Albert, died in Mexico, possibly of typhus, a few weeks later.

Lou continued to live a life of high-society impoverishment, reflecting in a letter to André Rouveyre that she really had been that 'wild and unbearable animal' and Apollinaire had been good, sensitive and stylish.[1] She died in 1963 and is buried in Passy cemetery in Paris. From the 1940s some of the poet's letters to her began to emerge, but an attempt in the 1950s to publish a comprehensive facsimile proved premature. Only in 1969 did the first edition of *Lettres à Lou* finally become available.

Madeleine never married. She taught at a girls' secondary school in Saint-Cloud, then in Nice from 1949, and was fondly remembered by many former pupils. She died in Antibes in March 1965. Madeleine sanctioned the publication of an edited version of Apollinaire's letters to her entitled *Tendre comme le souvenir* in 1952 and supplied a short memoir of her first meeting with him. A full edition, including Apollinaire's more explicit letters and poems, appeared only in 2005.

Jacqueline Apollinaire, or Ruby, received a small pension because her husband had officially 'died for France'. She did not remarry and devoted herself to managing her husband's reputation

and papers. She was buried with Apollinaire in Père-Lachaise cemetery in 1967. Her relatives still attend an annual gathering of
Apollinaire scholars and enthusiasts and recite his poems.

As for Apollinaire's other loves, Annie Playden emigrated to
America, where many years later she was tracked down by Apollinaire scholars. She had no inkling that the young man she had
known as Kostro had become a world-famous poet. Marie
Laurencin divorced her German husband in 1920 and returned to
Paris, where she painted portraits of society figures as well as sets
for the theatre and ballet.

NOTES

Prelude: Paris, 1914

1. In fact, Apollinaire had published a violently pornographic novel, *Les Onze mille verges* (*The Eleven Thousand Rods*), in 1907 but only signed it G.A. A translation by Nina Rootes is available as a Peter Owen Modern Classic.

Postlude: Paris, November 1918

1. See Laurence Campa, *Guillaume Apollinaire*, Paris: Gallimard, 2013, p. 764.
2. The influenza came in waves, appearing first in spring 1918 in US military camps. For a discussion of the impact of the epidemic, see Annette Becker, *Guillaume Apollinaire: Une biographie de guerre*, Paris: Tallandier, 2009, pp. 204–12.
3. Jacqueline Peltier has imaginatively re-created the last few days of the poet's life in *Apollinaire: Poet of War and Peace*, London: Cecil Woolf Publishers, 2012.
4. See Louise Faure-Favier, *Souvenirs sur Apollinaire*, Paris: Grasset, 1945, pp. 206–7. Becker, p. 208, quotes a letter from Angelica on the day following Apollinaire's death in which she refers to Jacqueline as a harpy he had been stupid to marry.
5. The official notification announcing his promotion with effect from 28 July 1918 was published on 12 November. The poet was originally buried in a temporary plot before being moved to his

current position in Père-Lachaise during 1920. See Campa, *Guillaume Apollinaire*, pp. 765–9.

6. While Britain mourned a 'lost generation' of political leaders, France lamented the loss of its future intellectuals and writers. See Becker, p. 219.

7. The original poem is in traditional twelve-syllable alexandrines and rhymed. The last three lines form an acrostic, the first letters of which spell out the word LOU. Baratier was the name of the villa near Nice where the addressee of the poem, the poet's lover Lou, was living. For a concise introduction to French versification, see David Hunter, *Understanding French Verse: A Guide for Singers*, New York: Oxford University Press, 2005.

8. See Peter Read, *Picasso and Apollinaire: The Persistence of Memory*, Berkeley: University of California Press, 2008. Professor Read has also explored Apollinaire's work as a pornographer and editor of the works of de Sade and other writers of erotica in 'Apollinaire's Voluptuous Calvary' in Lorna Milne and Mary Orr (eds), *Narratives of French Modernity*, Bern: Peter Lang, 2011, pp. 47–66.

9. Laurence Campa, in *Poètes de la Grande Guerre*, Paris: Éditions Classiques Garnier, 2010, p. 44, suggests that it is only since the early part of the twenty-first century that Apollinaire has been considered *the* French poet of the Great War.

10. As Paul Fussell, among others, has pointed out, few of the literary modernists writing in English, such as Joyce, Eliot or Pound, had any direct experience of the war. See Paul Fussell, *The Great War and Modern Memory*, Oxford: Oxford University Press, 1979, p. 174. Exceptions include Ford Madox Ford (*Parade's End*) and David Jones (*In Parenthesis*).

Chapter 1: Deauville, Paris, Nice, August–December 1914

1. The three chapters of the novel found in the poet's papers were in an envelope marked with this title. However, the contract

Apollinaire signed with the publishers Briffaut used the title *La Dame blanche des Hohenzollern*.

2. In reality Apollinaire remained unconvinced about the rumours of war until quite late on. He wrote to his friend Serge Férat on 29 July, 'People are very worried about the war. Almost everyone is clearing out. I don't believe any of it myself.' See *Œuvres complètes de Guillaume Apollinaire*, Vol. IV, Michel Décaudin (ed.), Paris: Balland-Lecat, 1966, p. 780.

3. According to André Rouveyre, Apollinaire wrote his *Comœdia* article during this halt in Fontainebleau. See André Rouveyre, *Apollinaire*, Paris: Gallimard, 1945, p. 14. Unlike Britain, which had a small professional army, the French relied on mobilizing a mass of citizens who had previously been through a period of military training. Mobilization was declared at 3.45 p.m. on 1 August 1914 with effect from the following day. Germany formally declared war on France on 3 August.

4. Gabriel Chevallier speaks of wild merrymaking on the night after mobilization was announced in his novel *La Peur*, translated into English as *Fear* (Malcolm Imrie, tr.), London: Serpent's Tail, 2012, p. 5.

5. See http://www.wiu.edu/Apollinaire/Apollinaire_dit.htm. There is also no mention – perhaps not surprisingly – that the party on the night of 1 August involved smoking opium. The name of Rouveyre's driver is also changed from Nolland to Nolent in Apollinaire's retelling of the story.

6. The translation is by Beverley Bie Brahic.

7. One of the ideas prevalent in Europe before 1914 was that war would have the effect of purifying and renewing Western civilization, freeing it from a hidebound status quo. See, for instance, Tim Kendall, *Modern English War Poetry*, Oxford: Oxford University Press, 2009, p. 32, on Kipling's letters.

8. In its references to elements such as aeroplanes and blacksmiths,

the poem can be said to presage the mix of the modern and the atavistic that would characterize the conflict. See Becker, p. 21.

9. In a letter to Francis Picabia on 20 December 1914 Apollinaire wrote, 'I could have gone to Spain with a friend (Robert Mortier) who offered me the most generous and luxurious welcome there . . . But I couldn't have left France in such dishonourable conditions for a man.' See *Œuvres complètes*, Vol. IV, p. 848. He was highly critical of his former friend, the artist Robert Delaunay, who fled France with his wife Sonia, referring to him as a 'simultaneist deserter'. See Becker, p. 46.

10. A law promulgated on 5 August 1914 allowed the government to naturalize all foreigners signing up for the duration of the war. See Campa, *Guillaume Apollinaire*, pp. 507–8.

11. As Campa points out (*Guillaume Apollinaire*, p. 509), there are some unexplained questions about Apollinaire's approach. Why did he not attempt to sign up for the Foreign Legion, for instance? Did he think his naturalization would be facilitated by joining a unit of the regular army? Was he worried about drawing attention to his status as a foreigner?

12. The government would not return to Paris until 22 December 1914.

13. *Souvenirs de la Grande Guerre par Guillaume Apollinaire*, Pierre Caizergues (ed.), Montpellier: Fata Morgana, 1980, p. 21.

14. *Souvenirs de la Grande Guerre*, p. 8. Apollinaire continued to be short of money throughout his military service. In December 1914, for instance, he wrote to his friend Picabia suggesting that he send him fifty francs each month until the poet went to the front. See *Œuvres complètes*, Vol. IV, p. 848. After his return to Paris in 1916 Apollinaire continued to do various pieces of freelance journalism to supplement his income.

15. The relationship between Apollinaire and Marie Laurencin had collapsed during 1912. In August 1913 they had both been part of

a holiday party to Normandy organized by their mutual friend Louise Faure-Favier, but Marie resisted any attempt at reconciliation.

16. Rouveyre, p. 27.

17. The poem was first published in *Alcools* in 1913 but is dated September 1911. It has a number of echoes of Verlaine's 'Le ciel est, par-dessus le toit', which was written in prison after his infamous attempt to shoot Rimbaud and his condemnation for sodomy. The *Mona Lisa* was eventually recovered from Italy, in December 1913, where it had been taken by an Italian nationalist protesting at Napoleon's plundering of Italian art treasures.

18. Apollinaire set out his side of the story and Picasso's role in it in a long letter to Madeleine Pagès on 30 July 1915. See Guillaume Apollinaire, *Lettres à Madeleine,* Laurence Campa (ed.), Paris: Gallimard, 2005, pp. 96–8.

19. Apollinaire had been writing articles critical of '*le germanisme*' from the early 1900s, despite having spent time in Germany and having a good knowledge of German literature and art. This view of German culture was shared by artists outside France. In his memoirs the British painter and author Wyndham Lewis contrasted the oppressive efficiency of the German Empire with the freedom of inefficient nations. See Wyndham Lewis, *Blasting and Bombardiering*, London: Calder and Boyars, 1967, p. 8.

20. Italy had declared war on Austria-Hungary in April 1915 but delayed declaring war on Germany until August of the following year. This long free-verse poem, of which only an extract is given, is one of Apollinaire's crudest and most propagandistic. It was published in the Italian journal *La Voce* in November 1915. The 75's refers to 75-millimetre field guns.

21. This view was reinforced by incidents such as the burning of Louvain Library by German troops in August 1914. German intellectuals and academics, meanwhile, condemned French

culture as frivolous and decadent. See Michael Howard, *The First World War*, Oxford: Oxford University Press, 2002, p. 47.

22. Hew Strachan has argued, for instance, that the return of Alsace and Lorraine meant little to many French people. See Hew Strachan, *The First World War*, Vol. I, Oxford: Oxford University Press, 2003, p. 28. In a letter to the Italian futurist Soffici, written on 10 August 1914, Apollinaire noted, 'Here there's enthusiasm everywhere but without excessive displays'. See *Œuvres complètes*, Vol. IV, p. 762.

23. See Apollinaire, *Lettres à Madeleine*, p. 93.

24. She features in the register of the *École d'aviation Deperdussin* based at Étampes in 1912. Laurence Campa suggests Lou combined tradition and modernity in a sexually alluring way. See Campa, *Guillaume Apollinaire*, p. 513.

25. Toutou is a familiar and childish term designating a good and faithful dog.

26. Guillaume Apollinaire, *Lettres à Lou*, Michel Décaudin and Laurence Campa (eds), Paris: Gallimard, 2010, p. 12. Even Lou's nickname offered opportunities for punning – with *loup* (wolf). Apollinaire uses this opportunity in one of his wartime poems.

27. Apollinaire described Borie in a letter to Madeleine Pagès as 'a charming and refined shirker who spends his time at home smoking opium and taking cocaine'. See Apollinaire, *Lettres à Madeleine*, p. 101. On 20 December 1914 Apollinaire wrote to his friend Fernand Fleuret that he had not had a moment free during his time in Nice: 'First opium, then love took up all my days and all my nights' (*Œuvres complètes*, Vol. IV, p. 746). However, the poet was never more than an occasional user of the drug.

28. André Rouveyre, who knew both Apollinaire and Lou well, suggests that she became involved in litigation with her mother over her inheritance after the death of her beloved father in 1913 (Rouveyre, p. 119). Despite his own precarious finances

Apollinaire sent Lou money during the war and let her stay in his flat in the boulevard Saint-Germain when she visited Paris.

29. Apollinaire's letter is actually dated 5 September, a sign perhaps of his distress.

30. See Laurence Campa, *Je pense à toi mon lou*, Paris: Les Éditions Textuel, 2007, p. 7.

31. This is a reference to the eleventh labour of Hercules.

32. The poet had not yet decided what to call them. In June 1914 he refers to the poems as '*idéogrammes lyriques*'. He later settled on the term '*calligrammes*'. The word comes from a combination of the Greek words for 'beauty' and 'letter' and therefore underlines the visual aspects of these poems.

33. Lou and Mémée were working as volunteer nurses at this point. The poem in the shape of a palm tree was inscribed in a copy of *L'Hérésiarque et Cie*.

34. See, for instance, the poet's letter to his friend André Billy on 29 July 1918 (*Œuvres complètes*, Vol. IV, p. 778) in which he describes his calligrammes as 'an idealization of free-verse poetry and a honing of typographic detail in an era when typography is ending its career brilliantly, at the dawn of those new methods of reproduction – cinema and the gramophone'.

35. For a fuller discussion, see Claude Debon, *Guillaume Apollinaire après Alcools I*, Paris: Minard, 1981, pp. 29–41. Apollinaire had an ambivalent attitude towards the futurists. While he maintained contacts with Italian futurist artists and in 1913 produced a tract *L'Antitradition futuriste* at Marinetti's request, he was also sceptical of the futurists' excesses and desire to create an artistic system.

Chapter 2: Nîmes, December 1914–April 1915 (Soldiering)

1. The total trench system would eventually run for around 750 kilometres from the Belgian coast to the Swiss border. The vast extent of the war effort is suggested by an estimate made by the

French in 1915 that for each kilometre of front-line trench there were more than twenty kilometres of other supporting trenches. See John Ellis, *Eye-Deep in Hell*, London: Penguin, 2002, p. 25.

2. See Strachan, p. 278.

3. The expectation that any war would be short meant that virtually no link had been made between military operations and industrial strategy. As a result, by the time the front line stabilized, 50 per cent of France's coal reserves, 64 per cent of its iron-ore production and 58 per cent of its steel-making capacity lay in German hands. See Leonard V. Smith, Stéphane Audoin-Rouzeau and Annette Becker, *France and the Great War 1914–1918*, Cambridge: Cambridge University Press, 2003, p. 62.

4. Literary figures were among the dead. Alain-Fournier, author of *Le Grand Meaulnes*, was killed on 22 September 1914, while Charles Péguy had died earlier the same month. On the German side the artist August Macke was killed in Champagne on 29 September.

5. *Œuvres complètes*, Vol. IV, p. 838. Capua is a reference to the luxurious life led by Hannibal's troops in the city, which is said to have undermined their battle-hardiness and contributed to their subsequent defeat.

6. Campa, *Guillaume Apollinaire*, p. 516, suggests that the authorities may have perceived that the poet had the requisite level of education for the artillery. The elitism and modernity of the service was potentially attractive to the poet, as was the fact that his grandfather had been a gunner. Joining the artillery also enabled him to avoid becoming an infantryman. The 38th Field Artillery Regiment was part of the 15th Artillery Brigade, 15th Army Corps.

7. Jacques Meyer in his classic book *Les Soldats de la Grande Guerre*, Paris: Hachette, 1966, p. 24, points out that the heavy losses in the field meant that the distinction between active and reserve regiments and young and old troops was quickly blurred.

8. The German Army had arguably a more effective blend of different types of gun, deploying 3,500 pieces of heavy artillery in 1914 compared with the French Army's total of 544 mainly obsolete guns. See Paul Strong and Sanders Marble, *Artillery in the Great War*, Barnsley: Pen and Sword Books, 2011, p. 11.

9. *L'offensive à outrance*, or extreme offensive, it was thought, would establish a psychological dominance over the enemy that would make up for any lack of physical equipment. One commentator has likened this to the tactics employed by the Dervishes of the Sudan (see Ellis, p. 3), although the idea was prevalent in all armies of the time.

10. A 1913 report for the French Army claimed that 'artillery does not prepare attacks, it supports them'. See Robert A. Doughty, *Pyrrhic Victory*, Cambridge, Massachusetts: Harvard University Press, 2008, p. 27. Richard Holmes in *Tommy*, London: HarperCollins, 2004, p. 398, argues that from the first days of the war it was clear that the future lay in indirect artillery fire (that is, where the gunners cannot directly see the target).

11. See Ian V. Hogg, *Allied Artillery of World War One*, Marlborough: Crowood Press, 1998, p. 35. The success of the 75-millimetre gun had negative consequences in the pre-war period, persuading senior military commanders that it would suit every circumstance and allowing politicians to avoid spending on other types of artillery.

12. In the event the number of 75-millimetre guns and, in particular, supplies of appropriate ammunition proved insufficient to meet the army's demands at the beginning of the war, and a hundred batteries of older and obsolete 90-millimetre de Bange cannon were brought into service in early 1915. The war diaries from the units in which Apollinaire served suggest that at least some of his time at the front was spent operating these older guns. However, the basic roles of the gunners and the dangers they faced would have been similar to those of the 75-millimetre crews.

13. Paul Lintier in *Ma pièce*, Paris: Librarie Plon, 1917, p. 193, describes riding on the limbers as 'a martyrdom. We're wracked by excruciating bowel pains.' Riding in the saddle was often little better. Apollinaire notes in a letter to Lou on 23 February 1915 that a particularly difficult horse has left him with 'a bloody behind for the last week'.

14. *Œuvres complètes*, Vol. IV, p. 822.

15. There were other dangers, too. For instance, there was always the possibility of a shell bursting in the gun itself, particularly as the French military had rapidly to subcontract shell production to private firms in order to meet demand, leading to a dip in the quality of the ammunition.

16. Meyer, p. 36.

17. During 1915 the millions of letters handled by the French Army were all routed through a single sorting office in Paris. See Ian Sumner, *They Shall Not Pass*, Barnsley: Pen and Sword Books, 2012, p. 72.

18. There was a concern among the High Command that spending time with their families would 'soften' the conscripts. *Paroles de poilus*, Jean-Pierre Guéno and Yves Laplume (eds), Paris: Librio, 1998, p. 88, cites the case of Marcel Garrigues, who did not get leave for the seventeen months he was at the front – it was always cancelled at the last moment. These practical problems played a part in the mutinies that spread through the French Army in 1917. In the wake of these mutinies, as well as ordering a number of exemplary executions, Pétain overhauled the army's leave arrangements, including organizing special transport for travelling soldiers. He also improved the food and rest areas. See Doughty, p. 363.

19. Being in the 'Huguenot city' of Nîmes did little to help. Apollinaire found that artillerymen were not well liked and thought the city had a 'poor spirit' (*Œuvres complètes*, Vol. IV,

p. 818). At one point he says that the Nîmois are like Dutchmen without the latters' bonhomie (ibid., p. 797).

20. Campa suggests that the ÉOR was an unofficial group established by the camp commander to promote a few favoured recruits. See Campa, *Guillaume Apollinaire*, p. 525.

21. In fact, Apollinaire had been strong in mathematics at school. See Campa, *Guillaume Apollinaire*, p. 32.

22. The training seems to have involved becoming familiar with a range of artillery pieces, not just the 75-millimetre gun. See his letter to the Mortiers on 17 January 1915 (*Œuvres complètes*, Vol. IV, pp. 823–4).

23. The poem is in regular eight-syllable lines. The stanzas have an ABABA rhyme pattern.

24. In a later letter to his friend Jean Mollet (*Œuvres complètes*, Vol. IV, p. 851) Apollinaire expressed his disappointment at not being promoted to corporal, as he had been promised on entering his officer training. He explained that a corporal had only to look after one horse, whereas a driver had to take care of two.

25. He also thought army life was toughening him up. 'I've become a first-class bastard,' he told the art dealer Paul Guillaume in March 1915 (*Œuvres complètes*, Vol. IV, p. 870).

26. Apollinaire's interpreter friend tells him that Nice and the whole of the Midi are full of spies who are trying to exploit the bad feeling in the south in order to foment revolt. Some of the army's suspicions can be explained by the unrest that took place when conscription was extended from two to three years in 1913 and which particularly affected regiments in the south of France. See Smith, Audoin-Rouzeau and Becker, p. 20.

27. See, for instance, Gabriel Chevallier's novel *Fear*, p. 234, in which troops from the south experience the north of France as a form of exile and argue it is not their country that has been attacked.

28. *Œuvres complètes*, Vol. IV, p. 851. He also told his friends the Mortiers that he was still dedicated to poetry (ibid., pp. 823–4).

29. There was a serious point to this anecdote. Spy fever was intense, particularly early in the war, and many people remained deeply suspicious of cubism.

30. Soldiering is my 'true vocation', he wrote to his friend Serge Férat in early January 1915 (*Œuvres complètes*, Vol. IV, pp. 780–1).

31. The poem is in free verse with no regular rhyme scheme. However, the two final lines rhyme (*espérance/France*).

32. Borys is Borie de la Merline.

33. On 29 December 1914, he noted, 'All the men in my dormitory, dormitory 33, want me to write a book for which they've come up with the title *Les poilus de la 33e*.' Apollinaire did not pursue the idea.

34. In February 1915 Apollinaire asked Rouveyre to send him three copies of his collection *Alcools*, which he planned to give to his senior officers (*Œuvres complètes*, Vol. IV, pp. 827–8). There also exists a letter from Apollinaire's friend André Level asking the regiment's colonel to give the poet time off from his military duties to work on literary projects. Not surprisingly this request was blocked. See Campa, *Guillaume Apollinaire*, p. 539.

Chapter 3: Nîmes, December 1914–April 1915 (Lou)

1. The poem mixes traditional twelve-syllable alexandrines with irregular lines. The rhyme scheme for the first ten lines has an AA BB pattern. There is some uncertainty over whether the letter in which this poem is included was written on 16 or 17 December 1914.

2. This is an extract from a longer poem. The poem again mixes some twelve-syllable alexandrines with a variety of irregular lines. The rhyme scheme follows an AABBCC pattern. The Tour Magne is a Roman fortification in Nîmes.

3. Apollinaire had a long-standing interest in all aspects of human sexuality. As well as editing a series of erotic classics, including

works by de Sade, and writing his own violently pornographic novel *Les Onze mille verges*, he had co-produced a catalogue of *L'Enfer de la Bibliothèque Nationale* (the library's collection of banned books). Letters from Apollinaire to his lawyer José Théry suggest that the poet may have met or at least been in contact with Leopold von Sacher-Masoch. See *Œuvres complètes*, Vol, IV, p. 921. Peter Read has explored the poet's interest in psychoanalysis in 'Apollinaire et le Docteur Vinchon', *Revue des Sciences Humaines*, No. 307, July–September 2012, pp. 35–59.

4. This poem is largely composed of twelve-syllable alexandrines. The rhyme scheme for the stanzas follows the pattern ABAB CDCD and so on.

5. This is an extract from a longer poem, which is in twelve-syllable alexandrines with a rhyme scheme ABAB CDCD and so on.

6. The poem is composed of twelve-syllable alexandrines, although some of the lines have irregular caesuras. The rhyme scheme is ABABA CDCDC EFEFE.

7. See, for instance, his letter of 14 January 1915 where he writes, 'You've had some verses the day before yesterday . . . Don't lose them, as I'll bring them together (the best ones) in a collection, and I don't have a copy of them because I write them direct.'

8. *Œuvres complètes*, Vol. IV, pp. 827 and 829.

9. Lou's anxiety about Toutou's well-being, particularly during January 1915, is a clear indication that French civilians were already well aware of the scale of the losses among French infantry.

10. Only a few of Lou's letters to Apollinaire have been published – see, for instance, Laurence Campa, *Poèmes à Lou*, Paris: Gallimard, 2005, pp. 163–6 – but they include one from 15 February 1915 where she seems to be acting out one of Apollinaire's erotic fantasies ('whip me . . . humiliate me') and another from 12 September 1915 where she asserts she is his little lou [*sic*] for ever. Campa cites work by Pierre Caizergues on

unpublished letters that underlines Lou's basic sincerity and honesty (ibid., p. 109, note 1).

11. There are hints that Mémée was not overly impressed by the poet, who at one point had to defend himself against criticism from both her and Lou that he had not doffed his kepi when greeting a woman in the street.

12. Apollinaire's italics.

13. Rouveyre, p. 202.

Chapter 4: Champagne, April–June 1915

1. Berthier had published a poem, *Grève*, in the Toulouse review *Les Facettes* in 1911. In November 1915 Apollinaire would publish an article on 'Les Poètes de ma batterie'. See Guillaume Apollinaire, *Œuvres en prose complètes*, Vol. III, Paris: Gallimard, Bibliothèque de la Pléiade, 1993, pp. 228–31.

2. *Œuvres complètes*, Vol. IV, p. 824.

3. British troops had similar experiences. Holmes, p. 271, notes how shocked new arrivals were at the emptiness of the battlefield.

4. In 1857, for instance, Napoleon III's War Ministry had purchased nearly ten thousand hectares of land north of Châlons in order to establish a military camp.

5. See Anthony Clayton, *Paths of Glory*, Cassell, London, 2003, pp. 62–3.

6. Doughty, p. 143, concludes that the attack had shown how enthusiastic action was no substitute for better tactics and weapons, in particular artillery.

7. According to Apollinaire he had come out near the top of his officer-training group in recent assessments and his commander tried to persuade him to remain at Nîmes, giving him his first stripe when it was clear the poet was intent on leaving for the front.

8. Speaking of the British Army, Holmes, p. 410, uses the terms 'gun line' and 'wagon line' to distinguish the forward and rear artillery positions.

8. Meyer, p. 70, also notes how many runners disappeared during their missions.

10. In a letter to Lou on 17 May, for instance, Apollinaire describes meeting a 'captain priest with his boots and cassock, underneath which he had his stole'. The poet is unsure whether to address him as Captain or Father.

11. Apollinaire was a great reader of cowboy stories and would later compare his camp to that of gold prospectors in California. Apollinaire's first major work, *L'Enchanteur pourrissant*, is set in a deep and magical Arthurian forest.

12. Apollinaire had always had a lot of contact with nature (for instance, during a stay in the Belgian Ardennes) but never in such precarious conditions. Life at the front heightened all the senses that had been dulled by urban life. See Claude Debon, *Calligrammes*, Paris: Gallimard, 2004, p. 74.

13. *Œuvres complètes*, Vol. IV, p. 821. The paradox of being able to hear birdsong even in the middle of battle is one frequently mentioned in Great War literature.

14. Guillaume Apollinaire, André Level, *Correspondance*, Brigitte Level (ed.), Paris: Lettres Modernes, 1976, p. 21. The letter is misdated by the poet.

15. Those in the French troops, including Apollinaire, typically used the word *boyau* to describe their communication trenches. The primary meaning of the word is an animal's intestine or gut. It is difficult to find an equivalent word in English to convey the sense of bloodiness and stench.

16. The German author Ernst Jünger, who served on the Champagne front in late 1914, described the communications trenches leading to the front line as 'white snakes' in his novel *Stahlgewittern* published in English as *Storm of Steel* (Michael Hoffmann, tr.), London: Penguin, 2004, p. 9.

17. This is the first stanza of a long poem in four parts. The first part is

in twelve-syllable alexandrines with a rhyme scheme ABABA CDCDC and so on. Elements of this poem, sent to Lou on 10 April 1915, were later incorporated into Apollinaire's poem 'La Nuit d'Avril 1915' ('April Night 1915') published in his 1918 collection *Calligrammes*.

18. Postal censorship was introduced in January 1915. Each of the French armies had three sections of between two and three men who read all letters to foreign addresses and another 500 letters per regiment per month. See Sumner, *They Shall Not Pass*, p. 77. According to Apollinaire's correspondence, for a period starting in August 1915 all the troops' letters were opened, but the army seems quickly to have reverted to its previous system.

19. Lou had already spent time in a war zone during her visits to Toutou, so Apollinaire may have felt less of a need to cover up the realities of military life.

20. German spotter planes were very effective. Lintier, *Ma pièce*, p. 144, comments that the Germans had become virtuosos in the use of aerial warfare. The Beaumont area where Apollinaire was stationed was heavily bombarded on 6 and 7 April, his first two days at the front.

21. The Germans first used gas in the sector north of Ypres on 22 April 1915. By the end of the month the French military authorities had begun distributing rudimentary masks, but the troops often improvised their own protection. For a fascinating discussion about references to gas in Apollinaire's poetry, see Peter Read's article 'Gaz toxiques et « larmes de rire » dans *Calligrammes*' in *Apollinaire au feu*, Péronne: Historial de la Grande Guerre, 2005, pp. 49–58.

22. Jünger, p. 172, claimed that the elemental forces of cold and wet were far more effective in breaking soldiers' resistance than an artillery bombardment.

23. Apollinaire speculates that the cause could be syphilis, but it seems

more likely to be gas gangrene, a condition for which there was no effective treatment until later in the war. See Ellis, pp. 112–14.

24. Holmes, p. 283. Henri Barbusse, in his novel *Le Feu*, published in English as *Under Fire* (Robin Buss, tr.), London: Penguin, 2003, p. 18, says the soldiers had become 'machines for waiting'.

25. Priests were not exempted from military service in the French Army, and many served at the front.

26. The population trapped in the occupied territories was subject to an increasingly brutal reign of terror during the war years, involving great physical and psychological hardship. See Smith, Audoin-Rouzeau and Becker, p. 43. British troops, of course, could fight knowing that their loved ones were safe, apart from the occasional German bombing raid.

27. Photographs and drawings of Apollinaire after his return to Paris in 1916 typically show him wearing his military uniform – a way of distinguishing himself from rear-area *embusqués*. His Croix de Guerre and the visible evidence of his head wound would also prove useful in facing down critics at some of the rowdier avant-garde events, such as the première of *Parade* on 18 May 1917 in Paris. See, for instance, Becker, p. 154.

28. Although, as Holmes suggests, p. 102, the use of conscription in the French Army meant that it had a wider mix of people and occupations than the British Army, at least in the early period of the war.

29. Rosalie was a nickname for the bayonet invented by the singer-songwriter and 'bard of the armies' Théodore Botrel.

30. These two stanzas are an extract from a longer poem sent to Lou on 15 April 1915. The longer lines are ten syllables and the shorter lines contain four. The rhyme scheme follows an ABAB CDCD pattern.

31. The few published letters include declarations of her love for him as late as September 1915.

32. A moratorium on rents had been introduced in August 1914.

33. Translation by Stephen Romer first published in 'Love and War', *Modern Poetry in Translation*, Series 3, No. 7, 2007. This is an extract from a longer poem sent to Lou on 6 April 1915. The lines are twelve-syllable alexandrines, although with some irregular caesuras. The rhyme scheme for the first part of the extract is AABBCC and so on. Apollinaire then changes the rhyme scheme in the second section of the poem to an AAABBB pattern.

34. This is an extract from a free-verse poem sent to Lou on 28 April 1915.

35. Part of a poem sent to Lou on 10 April 1915. This extract is in twelve-syllable alexandrines with an ABBAA rhyme pattern. There is a pun on A*lou*ette (skylark).

36. Part of a long poem sent to Lou on 15 May 1915. The two stanzas are composed of twelve-syllable alexandrines with a rhyme pattern ABBAAB CDCDCD.

37. The book was entitled *Tendre comme le souvenir* after a line in Apollinaire's poem 'À Madeleine'. The history of the volume was complicated by Madeleine's understandable reluctance to see the poet's more explicit poems and letters in print, among other concerns, and the full correspondence was published only in 2005 as *Lettres à Madeleine*. Even now, as the editor Laurence Campa notes, a number of texts are still unaccounted for, including Apollinaire's final letters to Madeleine in late 1916.

38. Apollinaire refers to Madeleine as a *professeur de lettres* or secondary-school teacher in his letter to her on 18 July 1915. However, her career was first as a *répétitrice* (language assistant) and then as an *institutrice* (junior-school teacher). See *Apollinaire (Revue d'études apollinariennes)*, Vol. 14, Clamart: Éditions Calliopées, November 2013, p. 29, note 14.

39. In a letter to Lou, in which he described the journey, Apollinaire was careful to leave the impression that both travellers were with him for the whole trip.

40. Apollinaire, *Lettres à Madeleine*, p. 13, in the *avant-propos* by Campa.

41. Ibid., p. 14.

42. Translation by Beverley Bie Brahic. The version of the poem given here is the one that Apollinaire included in *Calligrammes* under the title 'The English Inscription' ('L'Inscription anglaise'). This version makes some changes to the layout of the original poem (largely by inserting more line breaks) and omits Madeleine's name, which features three times in the original poem. The first mention is replaced by the words 'that apparition'; the second was placed after 'sweetest of names'; and the third after 'the touching name'.

43. See Debon, *Apollinaire après Alcools I*, pp. 138–9. From 1 June 1915 Apollinaire also took up once again his 'Vie anecdotique' column in the *Mercure de France*, although it did not appear on a regular basis.

44. Campa, *Guillaume Apollinaire*, p. 570, notes that local commanders would often allow the duplicating equipment that served to print military papers to be used for trench journals. The 45th battery's journal was named in honour of their British allies.

45. Although not a postcard that had actually been sent, so creating merely an illusion of reality. See Debon, *Apollinaire après Alcools I*, p. 155. SP stands for *secteur postal*, the sector in which a soldier was located for the purposes of delivering mail.

46. The version of the poem given here is the one that Apollinaire included in *Calligrammes*. This version suppresses the punctuation in the original poem but is otherwise identical. The translation is by Anne Hyde Greet.

47. The war diary for Apollinaire's artillery regiment suggests that it suffered badly in this area in the early stages of the war. Sumner, *They Shall Not Pass*, pp. 29–30, also refers to the French Army's terrible retreat from that part of France.

48. For an extended analysis of this poem, see Debon, *Apollinaire après Alcools I*, pp. 142–5, and Claude Debon, *Calligrammes dans tous ses états*, Paris: Éditions Calliopées, Paris, 2008, pp. 218–21. The version of the poem given here is the one that Apollinaire included in *Calligrammes*. This version makes some small changes to the layout and wording of the original poem. The translation is by Anne Hyde Greet.

49. In a short poem sent to André Billy on 26 April 1915 Apollinaire picks up his pun on Jarry's play *Ubu Roi*. 'I tell you, André Billy, that this war / is Obus-Roi (King-Shell) / much more tragic than Ubu, but hardly / Billy believe me / less burlesque, oh my friend, believe me, it's very comical'. See *Œuvres complètes*, Vol. IV, p. 775.

50. Peter Read has pointed out the puns and jokes created by the form in which many of these poems were sent. Apollinaire's poem 'À Madeleine' ('To Madeleine'), for instance, was written on a piece of paper shaped like an artillery shell – the modern equivalent of Cupid's bow. 'Le Palais du Tonnerre' ('The Thunder's Palace') was produced on the back cover of Tolstoy's *Resurrection*, making reference to the tomb-like trenches and martyred soldiers. See *L'Écriture en guerre de Guillaume Apollinaire*, Claude Debon (ed.), Éditions Calliopées, Paris, 2006, pp. 25–34.

Chapter 5: Champagne, July–November 1915

1. *Œuvres complètes*, Vol. IV, p. 865.

2. The area remains a waste land sealed off for use by the French military, which once every few years organizes a tour of the ruined villages – Hurlus, Perthes-lès-Hurlus, Le Mesnil-lès-Hurlus, Tahure, Ripont – that were ravaged by the war.

3. '*La guerre même supra-métallique, architonitruante*'. See his letter to Fernand Fleuret on 20 July 1915 (*Œuvres complètes*, Vol. IV, p. 749).

4. In a letter to Louise Faure-Favier's daughter Chérie, on 16 July

1915, Apollinaire commented that the French Army left it up to its members to organize their own shelters and sleeping arrangements. The letter gives a good idea of the improvisation required. 'I made a hole, with channels to siphon away the water, a drain, a big bed made of telephone wire and trellis. The door swings on the bottom of a bottle that I've dug into the soil.' See *Œuvres complètes*, Vol. IV, p. 793.

5. The poem is in free verse. The Decauville was a light railway used by the military to supply the front. Gavrinis is a small island in Brittany with a Neolithic burial chamber, the interior walls of which are covered in artwork.

6. *Œuvres complètes*, Vol. IV, p. 912.

7. See Clayton, *Paths of Glory*, p. 79.

8. See Apollinaire's letter to Madeleine on 2 September 1915.

9. *Œuvres complètes*, Vol. IV, p. 912.

10. *Œuvres complètes*, Vol. IV, p. 919.

11. *Œuvres complètes*, Vol. IV, p. 913.

12. Apollinaire uses the word *bobosses* in the seventh line of this poem and also in 'Les Soupirs du servant de Dakar' ('The Sighs of the Dakar Gunner'), quoted in Chapter 7. As Apollinaire explained in a letter to Madeleine on 4 June 1915, this familiar word, with the sense of hunchbacked, was used by artillerymen to describe the infantry with their enormous backpacks. Here we have used the word squaddies to catch something of the sympathy evoked for the 'poor bloody infantry'.

13. The flat trajectory of the French 75-millimetre gun was a particular disadvantage here, while continuing manufacturing flaws with shells led to a number of guns bursting and killing their crews. The description that follows draws heavily on Bernard Crochet, *L'Offensive de Champagne*, Louviers: Ysec, 2003. See also Campa, *Guillaume Apollinaire*, pp. 598–605.

14. Unfortunately, one of the effects of the rain and low cloud was to

limit aerial observation of the battlefield, constraining the effectiveness of the French artillery fire.

15. See Crochet, p. 65.

16. Contemporaries such as E. Alexander Powell, in his book *Vive la France*, Heinemann, London, 1916, also described this bombardment as the greatest the world had ever known.

17. All leave had been cancelled on 2 September and would remain so until early November.

18. *Œuvres complètes*, Vol. IV, p. 919.

19. The regimental war diary (*Journal des marches et opérations* or *JMO*) suggests this transfer actually happened on 2 November.

20. A slightly amended version of this free-verse poem appears in Apollinaire's *Calligrammes*. For Decauville, see note 5. Apollinaire uses the word *bourguignote* in the same stanza to describe his helmet, making reference to a type of helmet worn by infantry in the sixteenth century. It has been claimed that the Adrian helmet used by the French troops in the Great War was inspired by the shape of this more ancient design. Trenches, like dug-outs, were often given fanciful names, as the poem suggests.

21. German trench systems were widely admired by the Allies, while the French had a reputation for poor, almost temporary construction, at least in British eyes. However, the French High Command was under constant pressure to expel the invaders from its territory and wanted to give no sign that the troops were settling in for a long war. There was also a critical lack both of materials and labour on the French side. Moreover, the French adopted a policy of thinning out their front line in favour of more in-depth defence at an earlier stage than the British, who preferred to maintain a higher proportion of their troops close to the enemy. See Doughty, p. 254.

22. Translation by Beverley Bie Brahic. The extracts of this free-verse poem given here are based on the version of the poem that was

later included in *Calligrammes*, which incorporated one minor word change and some alterations to the formatting of the lines.

23. In July she admitted to being afraid of him. See Apollinaire's letter to her on 18 July 1915.

24. At one point Apollinaire asks Madeleine to be much more specific about which letter or poem she is referring to in her correspondence and not to be afraid of repetition.

25. Madeleine, meanwhile, was upset that Apollinaire was unwilling to broach the subject of their engagement with his mother Angelica.

26. Even in a correspondence notable for its extravagance Apollinaire's hyperbole is sometimes outrageous. On 17 September, for instance, he told Madeleine that 'I adore you, you who combine the sensuality of a Bacchante with the intellectual prowess of a Vittoria Colonna and the mystic ardour of a Santa Teresa.' Vittoria Colonna was an Italian noblewoman and poet to whom Michelangelo addressed some of his most passionate sonnets.

27. Laurence Campa makes the point in *Poèmes à Lou*, p. 52, that Apollinaire was not really a bohemian at heart, despite his immersion in artistic circles. Indeed, Apollinaire suggests at one point that duty is 'the underlying principle of social life, and without it mankind sinks very low'.

28. The nine doors are her two eyes, ears and nostrils, her mouth, vagina and anus. At one point, Apollinaire has to remind Madeleine that there are only nine, not ten as she has written. He had sent a similar poem to Lou earlier in the year, but, as Michel Décaudin suggests, the poem to Lou was one of memory whereas the poem to Madeleine is one of expectation. See Michel Décaudin, *Apollinaire*, Le Paris: Livre de Poche, 2002, p. 202.

29. Apollinaire would rework this poem to form 'Chef de section' ('Platoon Leader'), which appears in *Calligrammes*.

30. See Fussell, p. 231. Apollinaire, it can be argued, used eroticism as

a way of asserting how life should triumph over death and love over hate. See Norma Rinsler, 'The War Poems of Apollinaire', *French Studies*, Vol. XXV (2), April 1971, p. 175.

31. See Debon, *Apollinaire après Alcools I*, p. 164. Rouveyre, p. 88, writes of Apollinaire's relationship with Madeleine that it was like a well-kept fire based on very little fuel.

32. On 9 October Apollinaire wrote to her, 'You do me infinite honour by comparing me with Racine.'

33. Madeleine is reported to have confided in 1964 to Apollinaire's biographer Marcel Adéma that she would have been willing to become the poet's mistress. See *Apollinaire (Revue d'études apollinariennes)*, Vol. 14, p. 22.

34. Campa, in *Guillaume Apollinaire*, p. 606, quotes from letters from Madeleine to Apollinaire in which the young woman writes in a highly explicit and erotic way.

35. This is an extract from a longer free-verse poem. The poem is different from the work of the same title sent to Madeleine in early July.

36. Even this short extract contains a mixture of six-, eight-, ten- and twelve-syllable lines in the manner of La Fontaine.

37. The correspondence has been published as Guillaume Apollinaire, *Lettres à sa marraine 1915–1918*, Marcel Adéma (ed.), Paris: Gallimard, 1951, 1979.

38. She did eventually relent and send him a photograph but only in May 1918, some eight months after they had first met in Paris in mid-September 1917.

39. Apollinaire comments in a letter to Madeleine on 3 August 1915 that there are three well-known Polish writers in contemporary literature, but none uses Polish: Conrad writes in English, Pzybyzeswky in German and Apollinaire in French.

40. He does cite Cendrars as one of the best modern poets, but this

was shortly after Apollinaire had heard that Cendrars had lost an arm in the conflict.

41. This is reminiscent of the story of the poet Nerval being accused of having no religion. 'But I have countless!' he is said to have replied.

42. Meyer, p. 145, notes how abbreviations gave the administrative literature in the army an algebraic and hermetic quality.

Chapter 6: Champagne, November 1915–March 1916

1. Writing about the British Army in *Six Weeks*, London: Weidenfeld and Nicolson, 2010, p. 184, John Lewis-Stempel quotes a contemporary source saying that the infantry platoon commander would inevitably be killed or wounded sooner or later. The regimental war diary for the 96th Infantry Regiment recorded the death of Second Lieutenant Rolland on 31 October 1915 while leading an attack on a German trench, so Apollinaire may have been his replacement.

2. Apollinaire, Level, *Correspondance*, pp. 31–2.

3. On 24 November Apollinaire told Madeleine that his company had really distinguished itself at Tahure, site of one of the most bitter conflicts of the September 1915 offensive.

4. See undated letter to Eugène Montfort in *Œuvres completes*, Vol. IV, pp. 912–13.

5. This view would certainly have been shared by many front-line infantrymen on both sides of the conflict. Inadequate methods of communication and range spotting combined with the closeness of the front-line trenches meant that artillerymen frequently subjected their comrades to 'friendly fire'. In the German Army there was a saying: 'We Germans fear nothing but God and our own artillery.' German counter-battery fire had also proved so effective that French artillery units had to be positioned further back from the front line than pre-war doctrines would have

envisaged, making their support for the infantry much less visible. Paul Lintier, in a letter to a friend, spoke of being a shirker 'two kilometres from the Germans'. See *Le Tube 1233*, Paris: Librarie Plon, 1917, p. XVIII, note 2.

6. Toutou, of course, remained an artilleryman!

7. The battery's war diary for 15 December notes the deaths of three men (including Déportère) and the wounding of another.

8. Apollinaire actually stayed an extra night in the trenches on his first tour of duty in order to brief the troops taking over this part of the line.

9. Campa, *Guillaume Apollinaire*, p. 621, quotes a letter to Apollinaire from André Derain in which the painter commented that the horror of these hillsides scored with white trenches had no equivalent in any other parts of the front he had visited. Meyer, p. 74, speaks of the journey into the front line as a 'Calvary'.

10. Apollinaire, Level, *Correspondance*, p. 65.

11. On 5 December Apollinaire told Madeleine that a corpse on whose foot men had been hanging their kitbags had finally been taken away.

12. On 6 December enemy troops attacked the position. Apollinaire's unit escaped the main assault but was badly shelled. See Campa, *Guillaume Apollinaire*, p. 619.

13. The French, on the other hand, still relied on their 'little baskets with hand grenades', according to Apollinaire.

14. Meyer, p. 235, comments on how the life at the front led to a strange appearance of the unreal. Wyndham Lewis, p. 113, also uses the metaphor of the theatre, where all the lights have been lowered and an invisible orchestra is blaring away.

15. Apollinaire's sympathy for these young men is captured in his poem 'Bleuet' ('Cornflower', but also signifying a young soldier), which is addressed to a lad of twenty who has seen 'such atrocious things'. The poem was originally published in the June–July 1917

edition of the magazine *Nord-Sud* and was later reproduced in
Il y a, a posthumous collection of Apollinaire's poems issued in
1925. It was later set to music by Poulenc.

16. She retained a certain modesty, however, refusing to describe her
hips or anus.

17. The regimental war diary records bitter fighting on 7 and 8
December, in which Apollinaire's battalion was involved. Sixteen
men were killed and twenty-eight wounded over this two-day
period. On 20 December, during Apollinaire's next period in the
line, the war diary noted that the communications trenches were
almost unusable because of the rain.

18. The poem is in free verse. Memnon was an Ethiopian king, killed
by Achilles at Troy, whose statue was reputed to give out a noise
when touched by the first rays of the rising sun.

19. See *Apollinaire (Revue d'études apollinariennes)*, Vol. 14, pp. 19–40.

20. Lewis-Stempel, p. 94, writes about the British Army that officers
worked day and night, never stopping.

21. He seems to have retained this role until 25 January 1916.

22. The ceaseless activity can in part be explained by the appointment
of Joffre as Commander-in-Chief of the French forces in the
autumn of 1915 and his insistence on continuous training and
improvement within the army. See Doughty, pp. 254–5. Ian
Sumner points out that French troops were expected to make all
their own sanitary, sleeping and messing arrangements in the rest
areas and that periods spent there would involve a round of
inspections, guard duty, vaccinations, cleaning, cooking, washing,
lectures, parades, reviews and training exercises. See *French Poilu
1914–18*, Oxford: Osprey, 2009, p. 60.

23. An exchange of letters with André Level in early February 1916, for
instance, hints at a furious disagreement that both parties regretted.

24. The physical deprivations of army life, as well as the psychological
effects of the front (lack of colour, intrusive noise, the awful smell

and sights), commonly induced what the French called *le cafard* (blues). In *Le Tube 1233*, pp. 133–4, Lintier describes how this feeling would suddenly grab you and 'darken everything like a heavy black cloud'. Ellis, p. 176, describes how men's moods could go from enthusiasm to disillusionment in just a few months at the front.

25. The regimental war diary on 13 January 1916 notes the constitution of the 2nd Company of Brigade Machine Gunners with help from soldiers of the 96th Infantry Regiment.

26. In a letter to Madeleine on 10 February 1916 he claimed never to have time to write now, unlike his periods in the artillery and even in the front-line trenches.

27. The translation is by Anne Hyde Greet. See Debon, *Calligrammes dans tous ses états*, pp. 310–20, for a full discussion of the poem and its genesis. The version of the opening lines given here is the one that appeared in *Calligrammes* in 1918. The text sent to Madeleine was identical, but Apollinaire reworked the layout of the lines before final publication. A full version of the poem, in both French and English, is given in an appendix.

28. Breton and his fellow surrealists would later be highly critical of Apollinaire's aesthetics and his poetry, in part as a way of separating themselves from his legacy. For a detailed discussion, see Anna Boschetti, *La Poésie partout*, Paris: Seuil, 2001, pp. 236–43. At this point, however, Breton was very respectful.

29. The naturalization had not been easy to obtain, as there was no father and his mother was unable to prove her nationality. However, the army hierarchy had supported the application. See Campa, *Guillaume Apollinaire*, pp. 630 and 638.

30. The poet had fully expected to see further front-line service. In a letter to Madeleine on 18 February 1916 he described his unit as being part of a 'mobile division', adding that 'it's not for nothing that they'll have let the division have two months' rest.' Meyer,

p. 343, also comments that troops assumed any major period of rest was a prelude to a big attack.

31. Apollinaire kept the battered helmet for the rest of his life. Holmes, p. 480, points out that a soldier was lucky to be wounded during a quiet period, as the medical services were overwhelmed during major attacks.

32. Apollinaire's letters are confusing here, as he had suggested to both Madeleine and André Level on 19 March that the surgeons in the field hospital had been unsuccessful in removing the shrapnel embedded in his skull.

33. Examples can be found in *Les Dessins de Guillaume Apollinaire*, Claude Debon and Peter Read (eds), Paris: Buchet/Chastel, 2008. Apollinaire had been passionate about drawing since boyhood.

34. See Campa, *Guillaume Apollinaire*, p. 645 onwards. Madeleine's letters become increasingly heart-rending. In November 1916 she wrote that she was begging him on her knees to take pity on her.

Chapter 7: Paris, April 1916–November 1918

1. *Œuvres complètes*, Vol. IV, p. 765.

2. *Œuvres complètes*, Vol. IV, p. 766.

3. *Œuvres complètes*, Vol. IV, p. 914.

4. *Œuvres complètes*, Vol. IV, p. 766. Becker, pp. 160–1, suggests that the change in Apollinaire's character perceived by some of his friends on his return from the war was as much the result of his experience in the front line as of his head wound. Fussell, p. 90, has claimed that a person who has endured the worst of war is for ever set apart from everyone except his fellow soldiers.

5. His mother was not the only person with whom Apollinaire had difficulties. His return to Paris had allowed him to re-establish contact with Picasso, but the painter seemed distant and was busy collaborating with Cocteau, Satie, Massine and others on the ballet *Parade*. Apollinaire wrote to him on 15 December 1916, 'I

would be happy to meet you . . . in order finally to have a general chat about our characters, our grievances, in a word, our friendship.'

6. Apollinaire fulfilled the same role at Picasso's marriage to the ballet dancer Olga Khokhlova on 12 July 1918. He wrote a short poem linking both men's marriages to the war, which includes the lines: 'Our marriages are children / of this war, and triumphant'.

7. Translation by Beverley Bie Brahic. The early parts of the poem are in free verse, but this section is rhymed and in regular six-, eight- and twelve-syllable lines, with one three-syllable line.

8. See Campa, *Guillaume Apollinaire*, p. 657.

9. In fact, Apollinaire saw some artistic advantages in censorship. As he wrote to Madeleine on 11 August 1915, at a point when more rigorous censoring of soldiers' letters was being imposed, 'On reflection I told myself that the art of letter writing is going to be reborn because everyone will make an effort to write as best he can; they'll look for new ways of saying what needs to be guessed.'

10. By 1918 Apollinaire was working at the Ministry of War between 9 and 11.30 a.m. and from 3 to 6.30 p.m. daily excluding weekends. See Campa, *Guillaume Apollinaire*, p. 744. However, he still found time to host regular literary gatherings at the Café de Flore between 5 and 7 p.m. on Tuesday evenings.

11. Décaudin, *Apollinaire*, p. 62.

12. Campa, *Guillaume Apollinaire*, p. 651, suggests that the story was begun in early 1915, finished in June 1915 when the poet was at the front in the artillery and then retouched in the summer of 1916.

13. In Greek mythology Tiresias was a blind seer who was transformed into a woman for seven years.

14. In fact, Apollinaire had invented the term *sur-réaliste* around March 1917 and had used it for the first time in advance notes for

the ballet *Parade*, which had had its première on 18 May. His meaning was very different from the interpretation that the surrealists would later give to the term.

15. *Œuvres completes,* Vol. IV, p. 890. The organizer of the protest was, in fact, the art dealer Léonce Rosenberg, who felt that Apollinaire's play might destroy his efforts to make cubism respectable. See Campa, *Guillaume Apollinaire,* p. 700. Cubism – or kubism as it was sometimes disparagingly called – was highly controversial in wartime France, under attack in many parts of the artistic and critical establishment as 'foreign' and anti-French. The main dealer, Kahnweiler, was of German origin and remained in exile in Switzerland during the war. His collection in France was confiscated. When the British artist William Roberts applied to become a war artist working for the Canadian War Records Office he was advised that cubist work was 'inadmissible for the purpose'.

16. The issue would remain an important political concern in the post-war period. For a comprehensive and fascinating study of the play, see Peter Read, *Apollinaire et Les Mamelles de Tirésias*, Rennes: Presses Universitaires de Rennes, 2000.

17. The French initially mobilized workers of all types in August 1914. However, a number of skilled men were brought back from the front to work in the war industries. These men officially remained part of the army and could therefore be returned to the front at any time, making them more cautious about taking industrial action than their female counterparts.

18. Apollinaire, Level, *Correspondance*, pp. 49–50.

19. 'I am authoritarian, very authoritarian,' he wrote to Yves Blanc, 'but at the same time very gentle.'

20. Read, *Apollinaire et Les Mamelles de Tirésias*, p. 176. The play was later set to music by Poulenc, who also composed many songs based on Apollinaire's poems, including a number of those written

during the war. Poulenc's setting of *Bleuet* (see Chapter 6, note 15) is a particularly moving portrayal of a young man facing death at the front.

21. Note, however, Apollinaire's letter to Lou, written on 30 July 1915 from one of the worst parts of the front, in which he tells her that 'my gaiety increases from day to day, and I need all my strength to avoid bursting out in laughter, with the most painful laughter known to man'. Wyndham Lewis speaks of jests that were too deep for laughter. See Vincent Sherry (ed.), *The Cambridge Companion to the Literature of the First World War*, Cambridge: Cambridge University Press, 2005, p. 27. As Jill Fell also points out in *Alfred Jarry*, London: Reaktion Books, 2010, p. 175, Apollinaire was influenced by Jarry's play *Ubu Roi*, which has a savage humour.

22. Read, *Apollinaire et Les Mamelles de Tirésias*, p. 230.

23. *Vitam impedere mori*, a small volume containing six traditionally structured and rhymed poems of an elegiac nature and eight drawings by Rouveyre, had appeared at the end of 1917.

24. I am indebted to the work of Claude Debon in this section. See, in particular, Debon, *Calligrammes* and the wonderfully comprehensive *Calligrammes dans tous ses états*.

25. In the first part of 1914 Apollinaire finished a pantomime *À quelle heure un train partira-t-il pour Paris?* (*What Time Will a Train Leave for Paris?*) based on the poem 'Le Musicien de Saint-Merry'. There were plans to stage the work in New York in early 1915, but the project was shelved at the start of the war. See Décaudin, *Apollinaire*, pp. 166–7.

26. Translation by Beverley Bie Brahic. The poem is in free verse.

27. Translation by Beverley Bie Brahic. The poem is in regular eight-syllable lines with an ABAB CDCD rhyme scheme.

28. Translation by Beverley Bie Brahic. The poem is largely in free verse but with a few regular and rhymed lines. Lines ten and eleven contain a pun on *'jeter l'ancre'* (anchor) and *'l'encre* (ink)

que l'on jette. Lintier in *Ma pièce*, pp. 74–5, speaks of the noise of artillery being like that of 'the ocean during a tempest with the clashing of its waves, its breakers and its dull thuds'. Gas masks gave the soldiers the appearance of cephalopods.

29. Translation by Beverley Bie Brahic. The poem is in free verse. An earlier version was sent to Madeleine on 30 September 1915. TSF is a reference to *téléphonie sans fil* (wireless telephony). The poet's brother, Albert, was in Mexico.

30. The poem is in regular twelve-syllable rhymed alexandrines.

31. Translation by Beverley Bie Brahic. These parts of the poem are in free verse.

32. This lecture is an important statement of Apollinaire's views about poetry at this stage in his career. He argues for preserving the best of the classical heritage while encouraging experimentation, even if the latter sometimes leads nowhere. Freedom must therefore be complemented by order ('for France is averse to disorder'). He envisages a synthesis of the arts, where poetry will be found in everything from a galaxy to a single match being lit. Surprise is the mainspring of this new poetry, with the poet inventing new fables that inventors will then turn into truth. He concludes that 'Modern poets are thus creators, inventors and prophets' and the new spirit is that of 'the very time in which we are living'. As it was becoming increasingly apparent during the war that the next generation of poets and artists would violently reject the old, pre-war order Apollinaire's argument in favour of both experimentation *and* tradition was a controversial aesthetic position to take.

33. See his letter to André Billy on 29 July 1918 in *Œuvres complètes*, Vol. IV, p. 778.

34. To take one example, there are frequent references to invisibility in the poems, alluding to the unearthly emptiness of the battlefield, the continuing loss of men even in quiet periods at the front, the

increasing use of camouflage in military operations and perhaps even to wartime censorship.

35. Translation by Beverley Bie Brahic. This long poem is in free verse. The title may reflect the fanciful names often given to their dug-outs by the front-line troops, at the same time making an oblique reference to Zeus on Mount Olympus.

36. Debon, *Calligrammes*, p. 134.

37. All the poems addressed to Lou in *Calligrammes* were originally in *Case d'armons* or had also been copied to other correspondents. Until recently it was thought that Apollinaire had not been able to recover his poems directly from Lou (whereas Madeleine was assiduous in copying and returning to Apollinaire most – although not all – of the poems he had sent to her). However, Campa, *Guillaume Apollinaire*, p. 643, recounts that towards the end of 1916 Lou let Apollinaire know via an intermediary that his poems were in storage with other effects and that she would accept publication on condition that her name did not appear. Whether he was ultimately unable to retrieve the poems or whether he did retrieve them but simply chose not to use them remains unclear. I am grateful to Laurence Campa for this information.

38. We should remember that both these poems were originally destined for audiences outside France. In his letters to André Level Apollinaire argued on several occasions that France had to show a brave and resolute face to the outside world, in particular to the neutral countries.

39. Translation by Beverley Bie Brahic. The poem is in free verse. For 'squaddies' see Chapter 5, note 12.

40. David Jones makes extensive use of Welsh mythology in *In Parenthesis*.

41. The translation of both extracts is by Beverley Bie Brahic. This long poem is in free verse.

42. Debon, *Calligrammes*, p. 144.

43. Translation by Beverley Bie Brahic. The poem is in regular eight-syllable lines with a rhyme scheme ABAB CDCD. In the original French there is a word play on *Ah Dieu!* (Lord!) and *Adieu!* (Farewell!).

44. The word 'grenade' in 'Les Grenadines repentantes' ('The Repentant Grenadines'), for instance, can refer to the city Granada, the fruit, a hand-grenade or the female sexual organs.

45. There is an argument that only the deployment of such modernist literary techniques could fully capture the experience of a war that was perceived as chaotic, absurd, fragmented and ungraspable in its complexity and dimensions and in which the individual played an essentially passive and unheroic part – a bystander rather than an actor.

46. Quoted in Décaudin, *Apollinaire*, p. 129.

47. In fact, the *calligrammes* have presented publishers with real practical problems in various editions of the poems. How do you ensure the legibility of all the text and at the same time maintain the relationship between different elements of the image and the text? Apollinaire argued that the collection would require a superior page layout to that normally used in books of poetry.

48. For instance, the Scottish poets Edwin Morgan and Ian Hamilton Finlay.

49. Killed by a wound to the head!

50. Décaudin, *Apollinaire*, p. 177.

51. Campa, *Guillaume Apollinaire*, p. 684. The seated woman of the title refers to the image on a false coin.

52. Jacqueline was sent to Brittany in June 1918 in order to avoid the shells that were landing in Paris. Doughty, p. 453, has described the German attacks in 1918 as the darkest period of the war for the Western Powers, with the French seriously considering abandoning large areas of northern France.

53. The poem combines regular eight-syllable lines with no rhyme scheme, an appropriate mix of the traditional and the modern.

Epilogue

1. Campa, *Guillaume Apollinaire*, p. 781.

Tant d'explosifs sur le point **VIF!**

l'o^{se^s} guerre
tu en
si toujours
mot âme
un mon
Ecris *dans* feu
d'impacts le
points crache
Les féroce
troupeau
Ton

?

O M ÉG A PHO N E

COTTON IN YOUR EARS

So many explosives just about to be

ALIVE!

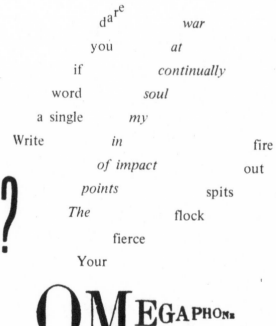

d^a^r^e   *war*

you   *at*

if   *continually*

word   *soul*

a single   *my*

Write   *in*   fire

of impact   out

?   *points*   spits

The   flock

fierce

Your

OMEGAPHONE

Ceux qui revenaient de la mort
En attendaient une pareille
Et tout ce qui venait du nord
Allait obscurcir le soleil

Mais que voulez-vous
c'est son sort
Allô la truie[1]

C'est quand sonnera le réveil

ALLÔ LA TRUIE

La sentinelle au long regard

La sentinelle au long regard

Et la cagnat s'appelait

LES CÉNOBITES

TRANQUILLES[2]

La sentinelle au long regard la sentinelle au large regard
Allô la truie

Tant et tant de coquelicots
D'où tant de sang a-t-il coulé
Qu'est-ce qu'il se met dans le coco
Bon sang de bois il s'est saoulé
Et sans pinard et sans tacot
Avec de l'eau
Allô la truie

Those who came back from death
Expected it the next time
And what came from the north
Almost obscured the sun

But what would you have
It's his fate
Come in the sow

That's when reveille will sound

COME IN THE SOW

The sentinel with the long gaze

The sentinel with the long gaze

And the dugout was called

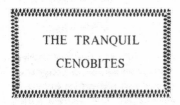

THE TRANQUIL

CENOBITES

The sentinel with the long gaze the sentinel with the lingering gaze
Come in the sow

So so many scarlet poppies
Where did all that blood come from
He's not half chugalugging
God bless the skunk he's rotten drunk
With no vino and no brandy
Just with water
Come in the sow

Le silence des phonographes
Mitrailleuses des cinémas
Tout l'échelon là-bas piaffe
Fleurs de feu des lueurs-frimas
Puisque le canon avait soif
  Allô la truie
Et les trajectoires cabrées
Trébuchements de soleils-nains
Sur tant de chansons déchirées

Il a l'Étoile du Benin[3]
Mais du singe en boîtes carrées
Crois-tu qu'il y aura la guerre
  Allô la truie
  Ah! s'il vous plaît
  Ami l'Anglais
  Ah! qu'il est laid
Ton frère ton frère ton frère de lait

  Et je mangeais du pain de Gênes
En respirant leurs gaz lacrymogènes
  Mets du coton dans tes oreilles
   D'siré

Puis ce fut cette fleur sans nom
A peine un souffle un souvenir
Quand s'en allèrent les canons
Au tour des roues heure à courir
La baleine a d'autres fanons
Éclatements qui nous fanons

Mais mets du coton dans tes oreilles
Évidemment les fanions
  Des signaleurs
   Allô la truie

 Ici la musique militaire joue
  Quelque chose

The hush of phonographs
Machine guns from the movies
The entire echelon is pacing up and down
Fire flowers of flashing sleet
Since the cannon was thirsty
        Come in the sow
And the trajectories bucked
And dwarf suns trembled
Over so many mangled songs

He has the Star of Benin
But bully beef in square tins
Do you think there'll be a war
        Come in the sow
    Ah! if you please
    Friend Englishman
    What a fester
Your brother your brother your foster brother

    I was nibbling almond cakes
While inhaling their tear gas
    Put cotton in your ears
            M'love

Then there rose that nameless flower
Scarcely a breath a memory
When the cannon went their way
At the wheels' turn an hour to run
The whale has other whalebones
Explosions we who fade

But put cotton in your ears
Obviously the flags
    Of signalmen
        Come in the sow

Here the military band plays
        Something

Et chacun se souvient d'une joue
        Rose
Parce que même les airs entraînants
Ont quelque chose de déchirant quand on les entend à la guerre

    Écoute s'il pleut écoute s'il pleut

puis	sol	des	con	la
é	dats	Flan	fon	pluie
cou	a	dres	dez-	si
tez	veu	à	vous	ten
tom	gles	l'	a	dre
ber	per	a	vec	la
la	dus	go	l'	pluie
pluie	par	nie	ho	si
si	mi	sous	ri	dou
ten	les	la	zon	ce
dre	che	pluie	beaux	
et	vaux	fi	ê	
si	de	ne	tres	
dou	fri	la	in	
ce	se	pluie	vi	
	sous	si	si	
	la	ten	bles	
	lu	dre	sous	
	ne	et	la	
	li	si	pluie	
	qui	dou	fi	
	de	ce	ne	

    Les longs boyaux où tu chemines
      Adieu les cagnats d'artilleurs
Tu retrouveras
La tranchée en première ligne
Les éléphants des pare-éclats[4]
Une girouette maligne[5]
Et les regards des guetteurs las
Qui veillent le silence insigne
    Ne vois-tu rien venir

And each one remembers a pink
             Cheek
Because even martial airs
Have something heartrending when you hear them at the war

Listen to it raining listen to it rain

then	bl	of	min	the
lis	ind	Flan	gle	rain
ten	sol	ders	with	so
to	diers	in	the	ten
the	lo	a	ho	der
rain	st	go	ri	the
fall	a	ny	zon	rain
ing	mong	un	beau	so
so	the	der	ti	gent
ten	che	the	ful	le
der	vaux	thi	in	
ly	de	n	vi	
and	fri	rain	si	
gent	se	the	ble	
ly	un	rain	be	
	der	so	ings	
	the	ten	un	
	li	der	der	
	qui	and	the	
	d	so	thi	
	mo	gent	n	
	on	le	rain	

The long trenches where you trudge
    Farewell dugouts of artillerymen
Once more you'll find
The front-line trench
The heaped-up elephant parapets
A mischievous weathercock
And weary look-out men
Brooding over the strange silence
    Don't you see anything coming

au
Pé
ris
co
pe

La balle qui froisse le silence
Les projectiles d'artillerie qui glissent
    Comme un fleuve aérien
Ne mettez plus de coton dans les oreilles
    Ça n'en vaut plus la peine
Mais appelez donc Napoléon sur la tour
    Allô

Le petit geste du fantassin qui se gratte au cou où les totos le
    démangent
La vague
    Dans les caves
    Dans les caves

---

1.   There was a wood in the battle zone called La Truie.

2.   Soldiers frequently put signs up at the entrance to their dug-outs. Cénobites is a wry reference to the soldiers' enforced chastity, deriving from an untranslatable pun: *laissez nos bites tranquilles* (leave our pricks alone).

3.   The Benin Star was a medal for colonial service.

4.   In a letter to Madelaeine on 2 December 1915 Apollinare noted that the anti-shrapnel earthworks were becoming more an more elephant-like in appearance.

5.   Weather vanes were used to monitor wind direction in case of gas attacks.

                    in
                    the
                    Pe
                    ris
                    co
                    pe

Bullet ruffling the silence
Artillery projectiles sliding past
            Like an aerial river
Put no more cotton in your ears
            It's no longer worthwhile
But call Napoleon on the tower
                    Contact

The slight gesture of the foot soldier scratching his neck where the
    lice bite
The wave
        To the cellars
    To the cellars

KEY DATES IN THE LIFE OF GUILLAUME APOLLINAIRE

1880   On 31 August the authorities in Rome are notified of the birth of a child on 26 (in reality 25) August. The father is unknown, and the mother wishes to remain anonymous. Angelica de Kostrowitzky formally acknowledges the boy Wilhelm (the future Apollinaire) as her son on 2 November.

1881–7   Apollinaire lives with his mother in various Italian cities. In June 1882 a second son, Albert, is born, also of an unknown father.

1887   Angelica arrives in Monaco with her two sons and settles there for reasons that remain obscure. The police register her in their records as a *'femme galante'*.

1888–95   In October 1888 Apollinaire and Albert begin their studies at the Collège Saint-Charles in Monaco. They will stay there until the college closes in 1895. Apollinaire is an excellent student, enthused by the arts but also by religion. He makes a number of lifelong friends during this time, including René Dupuy des Islettes, who will later take the pen-name René Dalize and to whom *Calligrammes* will be dedicated. He probably writes his first poems around 1892.

1896   Apollinaire spends a short period at the Collège Stanislas in Cannes but is expelled in May, possibly for having a banned book in his possession. At the start of the next school year he and his brother attend the Lycée de Nice. It is likely that Angelica meets her long-term companion Jules Weil during this year.

1897   At the end of the school year Apollinaire fails to obtain his *baccalauréat* and abandons his studies.

1898   A period of unemployment during which Apollinaire reads widely and sketches out poems and prose pieces.

1899   In early 1899 Angelica leaves Monaco with her two sons, arriving in Paris in April. Apollinaire frequents various libraries in the capital. Lack of money forces Angelica to travel to Spa in Belgium where she tries to gain admission to the casino. Her two sons spend much of the summer in nearby Stavelot. At the dead of night in early October they leave Stavelot without paying their bills in order to rejoin Angelica in Paris.

1900   Apollinaire continues to spend his time in libraries. He undertakes various pieces of hack writing as a way of earning money.

1901   His first published poems appear in the review *La Grande France* under the signature of Wilhelm Kostrowitzky. In May he is introduced to a rich German woman, Mme de Milhau, who engages him as tutor for her nine-year-old daughter Gabrielle. In August Apollinaire travels with Mme de Milhau to her properties in Germany near the Rhine. A young Englishwoman, Annie Playden, who is Gabrielle's governess, is also present, and Apollinaire falls in love with her.

1902   In the early part of the year Apollinaire travels around Germany with Mme de Milhau, Gabrielle and Annie. Apollinaire also visits Prague and Vienna on his own. He returns to Paris in August. Short stories, art criticism and further poems are published in *La Revue blanche* and *La Grande France*.

1903   He meets Alfred Jarry and André Salmon. In June he begins to work in a junior position at a bank in order to earn some money. In November he visits Annie in London. In the same month the first edition of *Le Festin d'Ésope* appears, a literary journal he has established with several friends.

1904   Angelica and her two sons move to Le Vésinet outside Paris. In May he makes a second visit to London to see Annie. The bank he is working for collapses, and in August the last edition of *Le Festin d'Ésope* is published. During this year he meets the painters Derain and Vlaminck.

1905   Apollinaire discovers that Annie has left for America. He meets Picasso and becomes a regular visitor to the Bateau Lavoir, where he also encounters Max Jacob and other literary and artistic figures. In May he publishes an article about Picasso and in September joins another bank, where he will stay until 1908. In December four of his poems are published in Paul Fort's review *Vers et prose*.

1906   Apollinaire tries to come to terms with Annie's departure. He works on his pornographic novel *Les Onze mille verges*, which is published clandestinely early the following year.

1907   In April he leaves his mother's home and establishes himself in Paris. He meets and begins an affair with the painter Marie Laurencin. He publishes a number of poems and short stories as well as an article on Matisse.

1908   He leaves the bank in order to make his living as a writer. He publishes a number of poems and writes a preface to a catalogue for an exhibition of Braque's paintings.

1909   He moves to Auteuil in Paris to be near Marie Laurencin. He contributes his first article (on de Sade) to a series on 'Les Maîtres de l'Amour' ('The Masters of Love') for the publishers Briffaut. In late November his first book, *L'Enchanteur pourrissant* (*The Rotting Magician*), is published.

1910   Apollinaire establishes himself fully as a professional journalist. In August his book of short stories, *L'Hérésiarque et Cie.*, is published. It is nominated for the Goncourt literary prize but fails to secure enough votes to win.

1911   In March *Le Bestiaire ou Cortège d'Orphée* is printed.

Apollinaire publishes his first 'La Vie anecdotique' column in the *Mercure de France*. He will retain this column until his death. On 25 August the *Mona Lisa* is stolen from the Louvre, and Apollinaire is implicated in the theft through his friendship with Géry Pieret. He is imprisoned from 7 to 12 September and viciously attacked in certain parts of the press.

1912   The case against Apollinaire is dismissed. In February the first edition of a new magazine edited by Apollinaire appears, *Les Soirées de Paris*. His affair with Marie Laurencin comes to an end. He signs the lease on an apartment at 202, boulevard Saint-Germain, which will be his home from early 1913 until his death. He works on a new collection of poetry, originally entitled *Eau de vie* but eventually called *Alcools* and meets the poet Blaise Cendrars for the first time.

1913   In January Apollinaire travels to Berlin with Robert Delaunay for an exhibition of the painter's work and contributes to the catalogue. His *Méditations esthétiques – Les Peintres cubistes* is published in March, and his major verse collection, *Alcools*, in April. During August he takes a holiday in Normandy with a group of friends. Marie Laurencin is one of the party, but she refuses any reconciliation with the poet. In December Apollinaire is one of twelve poets invited by a professor at the Sorbonne to make phonographic recordings of their work.

1914   Publication of 'Lettre-Océan', Apollinaire's first *idéogramme lyrique*, in *Les Soirées de Paris*. In June Marie Laurencin marries the German aristocrat and painter Otto von Wätjen. On 26 July Apollinaire and André Rouveyre arrive in Deauville to cover the season. They set off for Paris on the 31st, and mobilization is declared the following day. On 5 August Apollinaire tries to enlist, but on the 24th his application is deferred. He leaves Paris on 3 September, arriving in Nice on the 6th. After meeting Lou for the first time on 27 September he declares his love the next day. During October and November he takes trips with her to local beauty spots but becomes increasingly frustrated with Lou's lack of commitment, eventually deciding to make another attempt to enlist. After passing a medical he leaves for Nîmes on 6 December to join the 38th Field Artillery Regiment. Lou arrives in the city on the following day and stays until the 15th. On 31 December Apollinaire leaves Nîmes to spend a two-day leave with Lou in Nice.

1915   On 2 January he meets Madeleine Pagès on the train from Nice to Marseilles. On the 12th he joins an informal group of trainee reserve officers after a number of examinations. He spends the period from 23 to 25 January on leave with Lou in Nice. On 6 February Lou sets out to visit her male friend Toutou on the Argonne Front. During March Apollinaire requests a transfer to the front line. He spends a final leave with Lou in Marseilles on 28 March, during which time they pledge to remain friends. On 4 April Apollinaire leaves by train for the front, arriving in the Champagne region on the 6th and joining the rear unit of the 45th battery. He is appointed runner on 10 April and promoted to corporal on the 16th. On that same day he sends his first letter to Madeleine, receiving a reply on 4 May. Twenty-five copies of *Case d'armons* are printed on 17 June. At midnight on 27 June Apollinaire's battery sets out for the dangerous Hurlus area. The poet will remain in this part of the front until December. On 10 August he writes to Madeleine's mother, proposing marriage to her daughter. A few days later he receives a short poem from Yves Blanc and begins a correspondence with this 'war godmother'. At the end of the month he spends a week as a flash spotter, becoming a sergeant in command of a gun in the firing battery on 1 September. Between 22 September and 7 October he participates in the Second Battle of Champagne, and his battery moves forward into captured territory in early November. On the evening of 23 November he joins the 96th Infantry Regiment as a second lieutenant. From 28 November he spends eleven days in the front line. There is a further tour of duty in the front line from 18 December. On the evening of 22 December he departs to spend a period of leave with Madeleine and her family near Oran in Algeria.

1916   On 12 January Apollinaire arrives back at his regiment, which is resting at Damery. He commands his company temporarily and sends his last known letter to Lou on the 18th. In February the Germans launch an attack at Verdun. Apollinaire's regiment moves between various locations in the Champagne area, going back into the front line near Bois des Buttes on 14 March. He hears of his naturalization as a French citizen on that day. On 17 March he is injured in the head by a shell fragment, evacuated and operated on that night. By the 20th he is at the main hospital at Château-Thierry and on 28 March begins the move to Val-de-Grâce hospital in Paris. A further transfer on 9 April takes him to the Italian Government Hospital. He is trepanned on 9 May, an operation deemed successful. On 17 June he is awarded the Croix de Guerre. The British–French attack on the Somme begins on 1 July. Later that month Apollinaire is allowed to return to his apartment in Paris, but he continues to undergo daily hospital treatment until early 1917. In October *Le Poète assassiné* is published, and on 23 November he writes his last surviving letter to Madeleine. On 31 December he attends a banquet in his honour and is accompanied by Jacqueline Kolb.

1917   On 16 April the French launch the *Chemin des Dames* offensive. On 11 May Apollinaire is declared *inapte définitive*, absolving him from further front-line service. During May and June France is rocked by mutinies in the army and strikes on the home front. His oldest friend, René Dalize, is killed at the front on 7 May. In June Apollinaire is posted to the press bureau of the Ministry of War, where he works as a censor. On the 24th his play *Les Mamelles de Tirésias* is performed for the first time. Throughout the rest of the year he works on preparing his major volume of poems, *Calligrammes*. In November a small collection of verse, *Vitam impendere amori*, appears.

1918   Apollinaire is hospitalized with congestion of the lungs and requires treatment until the spring. In March the Germans launch their last great offensive of the war. April sees the publication of *Calligrammes*, and on 2 May Apollinaire and Jacqueline are married. Later in May he is assigned to the Ministry for the Colonies. By July the Western Allies have begun the counter-offensive that will eventually lead to the end of the war. In August Apollinaire and Jacqueline take a holiday in Brittany. In early November Apollinaire catches influenza and dies in the afternoon of 9 November at his apartment on boulevard Saint-Germain. He is buried in Père-Lachaise Cemetery on the 13th. On the previous day the official announcement of his retrospective promotion to first lieutenant is published. The première of *Couleur du Temps* goes ahead on 24 November.

1919   Apollinaire's mother Angelica dies of influenza on 7 March, just five days after her long-term partner Jules Weil has succumbed to the same illness. Apollinaire's brother Albert dies a few weeks later in Mexico, possibly of typhus, while Jacqueline, Lou and Madeleine all survive into the 1960s.

FURTHER READING AND BIBLIOGRAPHY

Apollinaire's complete works have been published in French by Gallimard in its 'Bibliothèque de la Pléiade' series. There is a single volume of poetry and three volumes of prose.

Gallimard has published the letters and poems to Lou in *Lettres à Lou* with a preface and notes by Michel Décaudin and additional material by Laurence Campa. The most recent edition appeared in 2010. Campa is also the editor of *Lettres à Madeleine*, again published by Gallimard, which originally appeared in 2005 and can now be purchased in a more compact Folio edition. An English translation of these letters and poems by Donald Nicholson-Smith is available as *Letters to Madeleine* (Seagull Books, 2010). Apollinaire's letters to his 'war godmother', Yves Blanc, have been published as *Lettres à sa marraine 1915–1918* (Gallimard, 1979), edited by Marcel Adéma.

Beverley Bie Brahic has produced a very attractive, award-winning selection of translations, mainly of the wartime poems, in *The Little Auto* (CB Editions, 2012). Anne Hyde Greet's translation of the collection *Calligrammes* was originally published in 1980 but was reissued by the University of California Press in 2004. Oliver Bernard has translated a selection of poems from across Apollinaire's work in *Guillaume Apollinaire – Selected Poems* (Anvil Press Poetry, 2004). Robert Chandler has produced a similar selection for Everyman's Poetry in an edition originally published in 2000. Meanwhile, Stephen Romer has published a small number of translations of individual poems in his own collection *Yellow Studio* (Carcanet, 2008) and in Series 3, No. 7 of *Modern Poetry in Translation* (2007).

The doyen of Apollinaire studies until his death in 2004 was Michel Décaudin, whose *Apollinaire*, published in French by Le Livre de Poche in 2002, offers a good general overview of the poet and his work. Claude Debon's *Calligrammes de Guillaume Apollinaire*, published by Gallimard in 2004 in their Foliothèque series, is an excellent introduction to the collection. Peter Read's *Apollinaire et Les Mamelles de Tirésias* (Presses Universitaires de Rennes, 2000) is a comprehensive study of the play.

As for biographies of Apollinaire in English, Francis Steegmuller's *Apollinaire: Poet among the Painters*, published by Penguin, is very readable but originally appeared in 1963. Also in English, Jacqueline Peltier has produced a short but very evocative and imaginative monograph on Apollinaire as a war poet in *Apollinaire: Poet of War and Peace* (2012), available from Cecil Woolf Publishers. For many years there was no modern biography in French, but Laurence Campa's comprehensive *Guillaume Apollinaire*, issued by Gallimard in 2013, can now be considered the standard work. It includes much original research on the poet's life during the Great War, building on earlier work on the poet's war years by Claude Debon in such books as *Guillaume Apollinaire après Alcools I* (Minard, 1981). Annette Becker's *Apollinaire: Une biographie de guerre* (Tallandier, 2009) also focuses on the period of the war.

There are many general military histories of the Great War but relatively little in English about the French involvement in the conflict. Robert A. Doughty's *Pyrrhic Victory* (Harvard University Press, 2005) examines in detail French strategy and operations during the war. Anthony Clayton in *Paths of Glory* (Cassell, 2003) and Ian Sumner in *They Shall Not Pass* (Pen and Sword Books, 2012) both focus on the experience of French troops between 1914 and 1918.

Finally, there is a great deal of wider material on Apollinaire. In English, Peter Read's exploration of the relationship between painter and poet in *Picasso and Apollinaire* (University of California Press, 2008) is particularly engaging. In French, Laurence Campa and Michel Décaudin's *Passion Apollinaire* (Les Éditions Textuel, 2004) and the catalogue for the exhibition *Apollinaire au feu* (Historial de la Grande Guerre, 2005) both contain wonderful sets of images from Apollinaire's life, while Claude Debon's *Calligrammes dans tous ses états* (Éditions Calliopées, 2008) and Laurence Campa's *Je pense à toi mon lou* (Les Éditions Textuel, 2007) examine individual letters and poems in fascinating detail, aided by facsimiles of the originals. The review *Apollinaire*, published twice-yearly in French by Éditions Calliopées, is an excellent way of keeping in touch with the latest scholarship about the poet.

Works by Apollinaire

Correspondance Guillaume Apollinaire, André Level, Brigitte Level (ed.), Paris: Lettres Modernes, 1976

Les Onze mille verges (*The Eleven Thousand Rods*), Nina Rootes (tr.), London: Peter Owen, 1976

Lettres à Lou, Michel Décaudin and Laurence Campa (eds), Paris: Gallimard, 2010

Lettres à Madeleine. Tendre comme le souvenir, Laurence Campa (ed.), Paris: Gallimard, 2005

Lettres à sa marraine 1915–1918, Marcel Adéma (ed.), Paris: Gallimard, 1951, 1979

Œuvres complètes de Guillaume Apollinaire, Vol. IV, Michel Décaudin (ed.), Paris: Balland-Lecat, Paris, 1966

Œuvres en prose complètes, Vols. I–III, Michel Décaudin and Pierre Caizergues (eds), Paris: Gallimard, Bibliothèque de la Pléiade, 1977, 1991,1993

Œuvres poétiques, Marcel Adéma and Michel Décaudin (eds), Paris: Gallimard, Bibliothèque de la Pléiade, 1965

Souvenirs de la Grande Guerre, Pierre Caizergues (ed.), Montpellier: Fata Morgana, 1980

Apollinaire in translation

Alcools, Donald Revell (tr.), Hanover: Wesleyan University Press, 1995

Apollinaire, Robert Chandler (tr.), London: Everyman's Poetry, 2000

Calligrammes, Anne Hyde Greet (tr.), Berkeley: University of California Press, 2004

Guillaume Apollinaire: Four Poems, Stephen Romer (tr.) in *Yellow Studio*, Manchester: Carcanet, 2008, pp. 43–8

Guillaume Apollinaire: Selected Poems, Oliver Bernard (tr.), London: Anvil Press, 2004

Guillaume Apollinaire: Seven Poems, Stephen Romer (tr.) in *Modern Poetry in Translation,* Series 3, No. 7, David and Helen Constantine (eds), 2007, pp. 18–26

Letters to Madeleine, Donald Nicholson-Smith (tr.), Calcutta: Seagull Books, 2010

The Little Auto, Beverley Bie Brahic (tr.), London: CB Editions, 2012

Other works

Apollinaire (Revue d'études apollinariennes), Vols 1–14, Clamart: Éditions Calliopées, 2007 onwards

Barbusse, Henri, *Under Fire (Le Feu)*, Robin Buss (tr.), London: Penguin, 2003

Becker, Annette, *Guillaume Apollinaire: Une biographie de guerre*, Paris: Tallandier, 2009

Boschetti, Anna, *La Poésie partout*, Paris: Seuil, 2001

Campa, Laurence and Michel Décaudin, *Passion Apollinaire*, Paris: Les Éditions Textuel, 2004

Campa, Laurence, *Poèmes à Lou de Guillaume Apollinaire*, Paris: Gallimard, 2005

——, *Je pense à toi mon lou*, Paris: Les Éditions Textuel, 2007

——, *Poètes de la Grande Guerre*, Paris: Éditions Classiques Garnier, 2010

——, *Guillaume Apollinaire*, Paris: Gallimard, 2013

Chevallier, Gabriel, *Fear (La Peur)*, Malcolm Imrie (tr.), London: Serpent's Tail, 2012

Clayton, Anthony, *Paths of Glory*, London: Cassell, 2003

Crochet, Bernard, *L'Offensive de Champagne*, Louviers: Ysec, 2003

Debon, Claude, *Guillaume Apollinaire après Alcools I*, Paris: Minard, 1981

——, *Calligrammes de Guillaume Apollinaire*, Paris: Gallimard, 2004

—— (ed.), *L'Écriture en guerre de Guillaume Apollinaire*, Paris: Éditions Calliopées, 2006

——, *Calligrammes dans tous ses états*, Paris: Éditions Calliopées, 2008

—— and Peter Read (eds), *Les Dessins de Guillaume Apollinaire*, Paris: Buchet/Chastel, 2008

Décaudin, Michel, *Alcools de Guillaume Apollinaire*, Paris: Gallimard, 1993

Décaudin, Michel, *Apollinaire*, Paris: Le Livre de Poche, 2002

Doughty, Robert A., *Pyrrhic Victory*, Cambridge, Massachusetts, Harvard University Press, 2008

Ellis, John, *Eye-Deep in Hell*, London: Penguin, 2002

Faure-Favier, Louise, *Souvenirs sur Apollinaire*, Paris: Grasset, 1945

Fussell, Paul, *The Great War and Modern Memory*, Oxford: Oxford University Press, 1979

Guéno, Jean-Pierre and Yves Laplume (eds), *Paroles de poilus*, Paris: Librio, 1998

Hogg, Ian V., *Allied Artillery of World War One*, Marlborough, Wiltshire: Crowood Press, 1998

Holmes, Richard, *Tommy*, London: HarperCollins, 2004

Howard, Michael, *The First World War*, Oxford: Oxford University Press, 2002

Jones, David, *In Parenthesis*, London: Faber and Faber, 2010

Jünger, Ernst, *Storm of Steel (Stahlgewittern)*, Michael Hoffmann (tr.), London: Penguin, 2004

Kendall, Tim, *Modern English War Poetry*, Oxford: Oxford University Press, 2009

Lewis, Wyndham, *Blasting and Bombardiering*, London: Calder and
　　Boyars, 1967
Lewis-Stempel, John, *Six Weeks*, London: Weidenfeld and Nicolson,
　　2010
Lintier, Paul, *Le Tube 1233*, Paris: Librarie Plon, 1917
Lintier, Paul, *Ma pièce*, Paris: Librarie Plon, 1917
Meyer, Jacques, *Les soldats de la Grande Guerre*, Paris: Hachette, 1966
Peltier, Jacqueline, *Apollinaire: Poet of War and Peace*, London: Cecil
　　Woolf Publishers, 2012
Powell, E. Alexander, *Vive la France*, London: Heinemann, 1916
Read, Peter, *Apollinaire et Les Mamelles de Tirésias*, Rennes: Presses
　　Universitaires de Rennes, 2000
——, *Picasso and Apollinaire: The Persistence of Memory*, Berkeley:
　　University of California Press, 2008
——, 'Gaz toxiques et « larmes de rire » dans *Calligrammes*', in
　　Apollinaire au feu, Péronne: Historial de la Grande Guerre, 2005
——, 'Apollinaire's Voluptuous Calvary' in Lorna Milne and Mary
　　Orr (eds), *Narratives of French Modernity*, Bern: Peter Lang, 2011,
　　pp. 47–66
——, 'Apollinaire et le Docteur Vinchon', *Revue des Sciences Humaines*,
　　No. 307, Lille, July–September 2012, pp. 35–59
Rinsler, Norma, 'The War Poems of Apollinaire', *French Studies*,
　　Vol. XXV (2), Oxford, April 1971, pp. 169–86
Rouveyre, André, *Apollinaire*, Paris: Gallimard, 1945
Sherry, Vincent (ed.), *The Cambridge Companion to the Literature
　　of the First World War*, Cambridge: Cambridge University Press,
　　2005
Smith, Leonard V., Stéphane Audoin-Rouzeau and Annette Becker,
　　France and the Great War 1914–1918, Cambridge: Cambridge
　　University Press, 2003
Steegmuller, Francis, *Apollinaire: Poet Among the Painters*, London:
　　Penguin, 1973

Strachan, Hew, *The First World War*, Vol. I, Oxford: Oxford University Press, 2003

Strong, Paul and Sanders Marble, *Artillery in the Great War*, Barnsley, South Yorkshire: Pen and Sword Books, 2011

Sumner, Ian, *French Poilu 1914–18*, Oxford: Osprey, 2009

Sumner, Ian, *They Shall Not Pass*, Barnsley, South Yorkshire: Pen and Sword Books, 2012

INDEX

Apollinaire's works are indexed by their French titles, cross-referenced from the English title where this is alphabetically distinct. Works by other writers/artists (except the *Mona Lisa*) appear as subheadings under the creator's name.

Page numbers in **bold** denote detailed analysis and/or extended quotation.

n = endnote

SOME AUTHORS WE HAVE PUBLISHED

James Agee • Bella Akhmadulina • Tariq Ali • Kenneth Allsop • Alfred Andersch
Guillaume Apollinaire • Machado de Assis • Miguel Angel Asturias • Duke of Bedford
Oliver Bernard • Thomas Blackburn • Jane Bowles • Paul Bowles • Richard Bradford
Ilse, Countess von Bredow • Lenny Bruce • Finn Carling • Blaise Cendrars • Marc Chagall
Giorgio de Chirico • Uno Chiyo • Hugo Claus • Jean Cocteau • Albert Cohen
Colette • Ithell Colquhoun • Richard Corson • Benedetto Croce • Margaret Crosland
e.e. cummings • Stig Dalager • Salvador Dalí • Osamu Dazai • Anita Desai
Charles Dickens • Bernard Diederich • Fabián Dobles • William Donaldson
Autran Dourado • Yuri Druzhnikov • Lawrence Durrell • Isabelle Eberhardt
Sergei Eisenstein • Shusaku Endo • Erté • Knut Faldbakken • Ida Fink
Wolfgang George Fischer • Nicholas Freeling • Philip Freund • Carlo Emilio Gadda
Rhea Galanaki • Salvador Garmendia • Michel Gauquelin • André Gide
Natalia Ginzburg • Jean Giono • Geoffrey Gorer • William Goyen • Julien Gracq
Sue Grafton • Robert Graves • Angela Green • Julien Green • George Grosz
Barbara Hardy • H.D. • Rayner Heppenstall • David Herbert • Gustaw Herling
Hermann Hesse • Shere Hite • Stewart Home • Abdullah Hussein • King Hussein of Jordan
Ruth Inglis • Grace Ingoldby • Yasushi Inoue • Hans Henny Jahnn • Karl Jaspers
Takeshi Kaiko • Jaan Kaplinski • Anna Kavan • Yasunuri Kawabata • Nikos Kazantzakis
Orhan Kemal • Christer Kihlman • James Kirkup • Paul Klee • James Laughlin
Patricia Laurent • Violette Leduc • Lee Seung-U • Vernon Lee • József Lengyel
Robert Liddell • Francisco García Lorca • Moura Lympany • Dacia Maraini
Marcel Marceau • André Maurois • Henri Michaux • Henry Miller • Miranda Miller
Marga Minco • Yukio Mishima • Quim Monzó • Margaret Morris • Angus Wolfe Murray
Atle Næss • Gérard de Nerval • Anaïs Nin • Yoko Ono • Uri Orlev • Wendy Owen
Arto Paasilinna • Marco Pallis • Oscar Parland • Boris Pasternak • Cesare Pavese
Milorad Pavic • Octavio Paz • Mervyn Peake • Carlos Pedretti • Dame Margery Perham
Graciliano Ramos • Jeremy Reed • Rodrigo Rey Rosa • Joseph Roth • Ken Russell
Marquis de Sade • Cora Sandel • Iván Sándor • George Santayana • May Sarton
Jean-Paul Sartre • Ferdinand de Saussure • Gerald Scarfe • Albert Schweitzer
George Bernard Shaw • Isaac Bashevis Singer • Patwant Singh • Edith Sitwell
Suzanne St Albans • Stevie Smith • C.P. Snow • Bengt Söderbergh
Vladimir Soloukhin • Natsume Soseki • Muriel Spark • Gertrude Stein • Bram Stoker
August Strindberg • Rabindranath Tagore • Tambimuttu • Elisabeth Russell Taylor
Emma Tennant • Anne Tibble • Roland Topor • Miloš Urban • Anne Valery
Peter Vansittart • José J. Veiga • Tarjei Vesaas • Noel Virtue • Max Weber
Edith Wharton • William Carlos Williams • Phyllis Willmott • G. Peter Winnington
Monique Wittig • A.B. Yehoshua • Marguerite Young
Fakhar Zaman • Alexander Zinoviev • Emile Zola

Peter Owen Publishers, 81 Ridge Road, London N8 9NP, UK
T + 44 (0)20 8350 1775 / F + 44 (0)20 8340 9488 / E info@peterowen.com
www.peterowen.com / @PeterOwenPubs
Independent publishers since 1951